The End

A Story of Truth

By

Adam Rudolph

ISBN-13: 978-1974293247
ISBN: 1974293246

Wrecking Balls Publishing
Key West, FL 33040

www.thewreckingblog.com

Death

This part of the story I'm going to call Death. I understand that it may seem counterintuitive to begin a story with something that is inherently an end, but as the Roman philosopher Seneca once said, "Every new beginning must come from some other beginning's end." And it is the most fitting word to describe this part of the story.

I never truly understood Death until that day. Ten days before his twenty-first birthday, a young man was lying in a hospital bed struggling with the possibility that his supposedly failed suicide attempt might just kill him after all. Two sides argued back and forth in his head. One was the voice of life, saying, "You are only twenty years old—it is not yet your time. You have a lot of life ahead of you still." The other was a voice of Death. A voice that had been ready to give up for years. A voice battered and beaten down.

This battle of life and Death was waged under a cloak of fear—fear that this may be the last day this young man and I would have together on this Earth.

One question kept running through my head.

Why?

Why would anyone, especially someone with seemingly so much going for him, want to kill himself? When something like this happens, it's a question inevitably asked time and again, but it's never really answered. Not in a way that resembles any sort of sense, anyway.

It took this young man's battle with life and Death to change that lack of an answer. At least for me.

His journey had been plagued with addiction and loss, the pages of his story written with pain and blood. The color in his world had disappeared long ago, and he had been wandering through his grayscale world, filled with a fear that he would be forever lost. Yet, amid uncertainty as to whether his life would be extinguished in a matter of only a few more days, the impossible seemed to happen. Truth was found. And the world gained light and color again, if only for a moment.

This young man turned to me in his darkest hour, a last-ditch effort to bring understanding to confusion, order to chaos.

He didn't want pity. He wasn't looking for sympathy. He didn't even really want help. He just wanted to find Truth. And share it with me.

As he put it, Truth meant understanding. Everybody has his or her own version of Truth, the version of reality that makes sense to him or her. If two people witness the same event, often they give two different accounts of what happened. Which one is true? Who's to say? Often, what we hold to be true is influenced greatly by our own point of view. And because of that, perhaps both versions are true—because both versions are true to the people telling them. But then again, maybe neither is true. Maybe the Truth is something abstract that we humans will never fully grasp because we are held back by our limited means of perception.

That's what he meant by Truth. And he felt the only path to peace and happiness was through finding your own Truth.

This dying young man taught me more about life and Death than all of the religions this world has ever spewed out. His unique journey gave him an insight on life that made him appear wise beyond his years. Maybe he was—maybe he wasn't. Maybe you'll begin reading this story and start judging. You'll start feeling pity or even contempt for him. These reactions could be quite justified, but they could also merely be involuntary.

I ask that you try to look past them, for although his has not been the most fortunate or the least fortunate journey, it has most definitely been a road less traveled. His last wish was that the insights he had gained from traveling this road would help somebody, somewhere, and make his or her path that much easier to traverse, if only slightly.

He had been part of my life for so long, and we had so much in common, that it's amazing to think that I didn't genuinely know him until that day. But this is not my story. This is his story. This is his Truth. And because of that, I will let him tell it to you. Rather, I will do my best to tell it to you the way he would have, from his point of view…

Pills

The faded red numbers on the alarm clock are blinking "6:33" in a blurry vortex between my half-open eyelids as the realization overtakes me.

I am dead.

"So there is an afterlife," I think, as my vision gradually clears and objects begin coming into view. I survey the area and realize I am in a familiar place.

This is my room in Boulder, Colorado. A typical college student's room. Dirty clothes and empty beer cans on top of empty pizza boxes on top of dirty clothes. The array is spread about in a way to almost suggest organized chaos, as if the garbage and dirty clothes are meant to be in the exact spots they are, and to take them away or move them would be to make the room look unnatural.

Disorientation rules my mind as it races aimlessly toward an unknown destination. Questions crash like a waterfall onto my brain, each one rapidly exploding into a dissipating spray, but none having enough time to get answered before another crashes down and splashes it into oblivion.

Is this the answer to that eternal question of whether or not there is an afterlife? Do the dead remain here on Earth, unseen to the living except for the occasional ghost sighting? Are all of those crazy ghost hunters right? Or maybe this is heaven, and instead of clouds and angels, it merely resembles the familiar places we had on Earth during our lives.

Curiosity takes control, and I decide to try and answer some of the questions hoarding my mind with a little exploration. My initial attempt at movement results in a feeling of being weightless, almost floating. I look down and see a fuzzy outline of my feet on the ground, but I can't feel my legs taking steps. It catches me off guard, and I stumble, reaching out to brace myself on the nearby desk to keep from falling over. This doesn't seem right.

Disorientation becomes confusion, becomes anxiety, becomes…

"Oh, shit."

The realization slams into me like a massive wrecking ball.

I am still alive.

I must be intoxicated from all those pills I swallowed. For a moment, "Oh, shit," becomes a sigh of relief.

I am still alive.

I am not dead.

But if I am not dead, I must still be dying. The relief becomes panic.

I am dying.

Wait. Why am I panicking? I did this to myself. I wanted this. I wanted to die. Granted, I really just wanted to go to sleep and not wake up. That was the plan. But I woke up. And now, I must be conscious for my Death. Is this why I am suddenly scared of dying? Or is it simply the natural human instinct for survival kicking in?

The only thing I could think about last night was finally ending it. It consumed my every thought. All I have been able to think about for a long time now is finally putting an end to this hell I've been living in for so long. Putting an end to the pain. What has changed? Where was the misstep?

Maybe I should just let the pills take their course.

Go back to sleep.

Not wake up again.

Finish what I started.

I lie back down on my bed and close my eyes. In an instant, I am in a small, cold, metallic room with one door. I walk through the door, but I am still in the same room. I go back through the door, and again, it is the same room. My terror levels spike. I can't get out. The nightmare I had last night is flooding back to me. I was trapped in this cold, empty room for all of eternity.

Alone.

This was my afterlife.

I open my eyes and sit up so fast that I almost fall out of bed. I don't ever want to go back to that room. The panic returns.

I'm dying.

Whatever it is that has changed my mind, it is not going away. I don't want to die anymore. I need help. But who—911? No. No fucking way. I'm not going back to that hospital, that ominous asylum of terror they took me to the night she found me bleeding. That night, she found me and didn't know what to do, so she called 911. I didn't blame her for it. I understood why she did it. But those idiots at that hospital didn't understand. And they never will. To them, I'm just another suicidal nut job. A blank face that serves as nothing more than a tedious addition to their workday. I'm not even a human being to them.

What do I do?

"Are you all right, man?" Adam's voice fills the air like a checkered flag for my racing mind.

I forgot he was here. I have felt a constant stinging of loneliness for so long that I can no longer tell when I am actually alone and when I'm not.

My house has been all but empty for several weeks now. My fraternity brothers all went home for summer break. As the house manager, I am tasked to stay here by myself and take care of the house until the fall semester when everybody will return. I don't mind, though. This house is the closest thing to a home I have known in a long time.

"No. I'm fucked up, man."

"What's going on?"

"I'm fucked up." I'm not sure why I just keep repeating myself. I guess I don't know what else to say. I don't know how to explain. My hands are shaking uncontrollably, and I fall back down when I attempt to stand up.

"What's going on, man?"

"I. I took a bunch of pills last night." As hard as I try not to, I keep slurring the words like an alcoholic in the depths of a binge. It's not just my hands or my speech. None of the muscles in my body want to work the way they normally do. My body is shutting down.

"What?"

"I need help."

Adam snatches the cell phone sitting on my desk and dials 911.

The house is silent enough and the phone loud enough for me to hear the operator on the other end:

"Hello, 911 Emergency."

"I need help…"

I start to zone out. It's better to just let Adam handle it from here. I still hear intermittent bits and pieces as I slowly slip away from reality.

"…shaking really badly…"

"…address?"

"We're at 1005…"

"…hang in there—I'm sending help now…"

Things are growing fainter now. My eyelids are getting heavy, and I sit back down on my bed. The shaking subsides a bit. It seems it is exacerbated by my attempts to use my muscles. As my mind relaxes, so do my twitching muscles.

I hear echoes in the background, but I can't really make them out anymore. I don't remember passing out. But who ever does? When I come to, I'm riding in an ambulance.

Fuck me. Off to that fucking hospital, I guess. Soon I'll be answering stupid question after stupid question. Soon I'll be bombarded with suggestions and advice that could only come from people who just don't get it—people that think they understand because they paid ungodly amounts of money to some college claiming to teach them how to understand. Classes taught by other dipshits that don't understand either. Because they did the same stupid shit just several years earlier.

I've never understood why the psychiatric and psychological field is filled with such complete morons. My mother always said that people go into that field to figure out what is wrong with themselves. From what I've seen, my diagnosis would be "stupidity."

Have you ever noticed that every single time you go to the doctor, they inevitably write you a prescription for something? They hand out pills for make-believe diseases like they're handing out candy.

"My kid doesn't pay attention in school."

"Okay, here's some legal speed that is almost identical in chemical structure to crystal meth. That will help your child focus."

Give me a fucking break. Anybody will focus better with a methamphetamine-like jolt to the nervous system. Why else would so many kids snort their Adderall like it's cocaine during exam weeks?

The kid doesn't pay attention in school because school is boring. All these so-called doctors and therapists are doing is making perfectly normal people think there is something wrong with them, so they and the pharmaceutical companies can profit from it.

"Everything is going to be all right, because we have a pill we can sell you to make it all better."

If there's one thing I've learned from my experience here, simply swallowing a pill won't make anything better. I guess swallowing forty pills doesn't either.

"Don't I know you?"

I look over at the paramedic that just spoke to me. She's older than me, late twenties, I would guess—blond hair, brown eyes, not ugly, but a bit plain…She does not invoke even a spark of familiarity in me at all.

"I don't think so," I reply.

"You worked at Viceroy, right? The ski area?"

Holy shit. This woman knows me. Just what I need—somebody that knows who I am, seeing me in this condition. Maybe it will get back to my friends and family, and they'll try to "save" me. They wouldn't understand how futile that would be. I am way beyond saving now.

"Yeah, I did."

"Thought so. I'm Jane. I used to be on ski patrol up there. You were a ski instructor, right?"

"Yeah, in the children's center. That was a long time ago, though."

"About two years, not that long," she retorts.

In the grand scheme of things, she's right. Two years isn't really all that long of a time. But two years to a twenty-year-old is an eternity.

Silence descends again as we run out of things to say. At least she doesn't really know me. I doubt we know very many (if any) of the same people now. I haven't been in touch with anybody I worked with at that ski area in years. Still, it's a little rattling, and a small part of me even wishes we were at that fucking hospital already. But there's a question that's been on my mind since I regained consciousness, something eating at me that maybe she knows the answer to. My need to ask overcomes my rattled condition,

"Jane?"

"Yeah?"

"Am I going to die?"

I think the question catches her off guard. Maybe it's the nonchalant way in which I asked. I imagine that question usually carries an emotional tone, asked by somebody afraid of an honest answer and probably looking for some comfort. I'm not scared. I'm not looking for comfort. I'm simply curious and want an honest answer. She hesitates for a moment before replying,

"We're going to help you. We're almost at the hospital."

Her reply, in turn, catches me off guard—also because it wasn't what I was expecting. I expected a rehearsed answer meant to calm fears and provide the aforementioned comfort.

I expected a lie.

I assumed she would say that everything was going to be all right even if she knew I was a goner. Maybe I've seen too many movies or just don't understand people as well as I think I do, but I really wasn't expecting that. She didn't say that I was going to die, but she didn't say that I was going to live either. I feel like I am interviewing a politician, the way she answered my question without really answering it. I guess it doesn't really matter. I'm still honestly not sure whether I want to live or die at this point anyway. Okay, that isn't true either. I still want to die. I just don't want to be conscious for it.

We arrive at the hospital, and they wheel me through the emergency-room entrance. It's not what you would expect to see. Television and movies would have you anticipating a very different scene. People are not bleeding in the lobby or screaming in the hallway for a doctor to help them. Medical personnel aren't rushing to my side, asking the paramedics all sorts of questions as if every second counts.

Rather, the paramedics calmly wheel me into a room near the entrance. A nurse casually follows us in and hooks me up to an IV. She warns me about the needle as per usual, but I don't even flinch as she inserts it into my arm. Physical pain has not bothered me for quite some time now. In fact, the infliction of pain sometimes gives me a shot of adrenaline that soothes me. As fucked up as that is.

A doctor enters the room shortly thereafter and commences asking me questions. I think he introduces himself first, but I don't really pay enough attention to know for sure. His name could be Dr. Dipshit for all I know. That works. That's what I'll call him from here on out.

"How many pills did you take?"

"About forty."

"When did you take them?"

"I don't know. A few hours ago. What time is it?"

"What kind of pills were they?"

"Sleeping pills."

"Were they prescription, or were they over the counter?"

"Over the counter."

"Did they contain Tylenol?"

"I don't know."

"Think. It's very important that we know exactly what you took so we know how to help you."

"What difference does it make?"

"Many over-the-counter sleeping aids contain Tylenol, or acetaminophen, and if that is the case, with the number of pills you took, you will need a liver transplant, or you will die."

Well, there's an answer to the question I posed to Jane a bit earlier.

"Can't you just pump my stomach or some shit?"

"That wouldn't work. It's been too long since you took them. They've already been absorbed into your bloodstream."

"How much time do I have, then?"

"I can't say without knowing what you took. But if it did contain acetaminophen, you have about three days of excruciating pain before you need the transplant."

"Well, that sounds like fun."

"Being so young, your chances of getting a liver are much better. The younger you are, the higher they bump you up on the list."

"Wait, let me get this straight. Even though I did this to myself, I'll get bumped ahead of somebody that needs a liver through no fault of their own—because I'm younger than they are?"

This didn't seem right to me.

"Correct. They weigh several factors: age, importance to community, things like that."

"So a politician or a lawyer or something will get bumped ahead of a garbage man?"

"Possibly."

"That's actually kind of fucked up."

"I don't make the rules. So, uh, back to the pills?"

"I honestly don't know what was in them. I took them out of the box and placed them all on a plate. I threw the box away. Then I swallowed them, chasing them with swigs of vodka."

"How much vodka did you drink?"

"After the pills or the whole day?"

"The whole day."

"Probably around three quarters of a handle. Why?"

"A handle? You mean the biggest bottles they sell?"

"Yeah."

"That's a ton of alcohol."

"Not really. Par for course for me."

"Well, the alcohol might actually help slow your absorption of the pills into the bloodstream. We're going to have to run some tests, see if we can figure out exactly what you took."

"Okay."

My mind wanders back to several days ago, when I bought the pills. I entered the grocery store intent on purchasing only one item. I had remembered hearing somewhere that Marilyn Monroe had killed herself with an overdose of sleeping pills. She just went to sleep and never woke up. That's how I wanted to go. I had endured enough pain. I didn't need any more.

I went straight back to the pharmacy section and began my search. I remember holding one box in my left hand that read TYLENOL PM across the front and a generic store brand in my right that read SLEEPING PILLS. They both had a warning on the back that read, IN THE EVENT OF OVERDOSE, CALL A PHYSICIAN IMMEDIATELY. I remember thinking that either one should suit my purpose, but for the life of me, literally, I cannot remember which box I ended up purchasing. They both could have contained acetaminophen, for all I know—in which case, it really doesn't matter which one I bought anyway.

Dr. Dipshit writes some notes on a clipboard and exits the room. It's not your typical hospital room. There are solid walls and a door on a hinge as opposed to a giant blue curtain. At least I'll have some semblance of privacy.

He leaves the door open. Never mind. So much for that notion.

From somewhere in the hospital, I can hear a bloodcurdling howl of pain. Have I mentioned just how much I hate hospitals yet? I close my eyes and try, quite unsuccessfully, to block it out. Then, out of nowhere, I hear a voice in the room. A lifeline.

"Fucking hell, would somebody give that guy some morphine or something already?"

I didn't even notice Adam come in. I guess there's a distinct possibility he was there the whole time. It's been a bit foggy as of late. I chuckle.

"Yeah, right?"

"How are you holding up, buddy?"

"Oh, just peachy."

"What did the doctor say?"

"That if the pills I took have Tylenol in them, I need a liver transplant within the next three days or I'm going to die an agonizingly painful Death."

"Fuck."

"Yeah."

Adam looks down and to the side in a way that suggests he has no idea what to say next. Adam has been part of my life for as long as I can remember. Yet, somehow, this side of me was not something he had ever been privy to. He was a fun-loving guy. He was always telling jokes, smiling, laughing. People liked Adam. He got along with just about everybody. He was constantly the life of the party. Even I had some fun when he was around. He was my polar opposite.

I know he doesn't understand this. It's hard for most people to really understand. Hell, I'm not sure I even completely understand it. I mean, when it comes down to it, it doesn't even remotely approach the vicinity of making any kind of logical sense.

I know he wants to ask the question. Places switched, I would want to ask it too.

Why?

What would make somebody try to take his own life? Yeah, I've had some bad things happen to me, but there are a lot of people out there that have it a lot rougher than I do. I'll admit, compared to many, my life really is not that bad. I'm sure there are people out there that would envy it, want it, even switch places with me, given the chance. It would be simple to explain if it had anything to do with the quality of one's life. The Truth, however, is so much more complicated than that. Or simpler, depending on how you look at it, I guess.

"I could try to explain it to you, but it's going to take a while."

Adam looks up as I answer the question he didn't even ask. "I've got time."

I take a deep breath, knowing that I am going to need it. "I'm not sure where to begin."

"How about the beginning?"

The beginning? Duh. That almost makes too much sense. But when was the beginning? I don't think I have ever really thought about it before. I think in silence for a few moments until it dawns on me. The Knife. It all started with the Knife. And I remember exactly when it made its first appearance.

"All right. I guess it started when I was about twelve years old…"

The Knife

"Are you going to the Lodge tonight?"

I didn't think I would have the mettle to get that question out. My voice was already shaking as if I had been standing naked in subzero temperatures for the past few hours. But somehow, I got it out.

"Because, I was wondering…if you are, that, maybe…you would like to go with me?"

The Lodge was the weekend hangout for twelve- and thirteen-year-olds in the small town where I grew up. It was nothing more than an old meeting hall with a stage built at one end. It looked like somebody started to convert a barn into a music venue, but stopped short somewhere in between piss poor and half-assed. Friday and Saturday nights, they would have a DJ, concessions, and, if the boys mustered the courage to ask the girls, dancing.

It had taken me two months to ask this question. I had been wanting to ask Jenn to go with me ever since the start of seventh grade, when I became old enough to go. This also happened to coincide with my learning of the Lodge's existence. In Truth, I had been wanting to ask Jenn to do something with me for years, as long as I could remember, really—ever since I first laid eyes on her.

Her skin was tan but somehow glowed with the subtlety and elegance of moonlight. I didn't think brown eyes could be that beautiful until I saw hers. The English language hasn't come up with words that adequately describe the peace I felt when I gazed into their shining depths. Her smile just melted your insides and must have had some disruptive electromagnetic qualities or something because I always had a hard time speaking whenever I saw it. More than all of that, though, and very unlike most beautiful girls I had come across, she was kind. She really listened to people when they spoke to her and provided intelligent responses. She listened to me. She was nice to me. At least up until now.

The Lodge seemed like it might be my window of opportunity. Yet, my balls would shrivel to risotto-sized pebbles of mush whenever I attempted to gather the courage to even talk to her. And when I finally did it, when I finally called her on the phone and asked her, her response was this:

"Um…"

To put it mildly, it wasn't the reaction I had been hoping for. I could feel my heart beating away in my feet; I didn't think it could sink any lower.

That thought lasted all of two seconds.

"So you like Jenn, huh?"

Heart took another dip.

The voice belonged to Brittany, one of Jenn's friends and a card-carrying member of the Cool Kids Club. She was just as pretty as Jenn but miles away from her degree of benevolence. And it appeared she was over at Jenn's house and was listening in on the call.

"What makes you think you are good enough for Jenn?"

There isn't really any reason to sugarcoat it.

Brittany was a cunt.

"Well, I…Could you just put Jenn back on the phone…please?"

"I don't think she wants to talk to you."

My mind was scrambling for words—words that could defuse this situation, put that bitch in her place, and allow me to recover at least a speck of dignity.

The perfect words.

They never came.

I had to say something, though. With every passing second of silence, my status as a complete loser was hardening in cement.

My mind flashed back to a few days before. I had revealed my grand plan to my friend Ethan. I guess I should have taken his lack of enthusiasm as a sign, but I was blinded by my ignorant daydreams of a Jenn that didn't exist. A Jenn that liked me. A Jenn that would want to be my girlfriend. I hadn't yet realized how others saw me. My perception of myself had not yet been tainted by the outside world. I believed my mother when she told me I was handsome. The actuality that ALL mothers think their sons are handsome, regardless of the Truth, had never crossed my mind. My friend Ethan knew better.

"Why don't you just ask to meet her there as friends?"

I hadn't understood at the time why he said this to me. Now, however, that ignorance was starting to fade away. His words were starting to make sense. Unfortunately, this didn't change the fact that I still needed words of my own. But they didn't come. So instead, I used Ethan's words:

"I was just wondering if she wanted to meet there as friends?"

I didn't want to be just friends. But it didn't matter anymore. At this point, I was in damage-control mode and attempting to salvage whatever shred of my dignity I might have left.

"Oh. Well, I don't know if we're going tonight."

"Okay, could you—"

Click.

The bitch hung up on me. I felt a ball of anger start to form in my gut. Who does she think she is? She's probably laughing at me.

Shit.

Jenn's probably laughing at me with her. And that's when I felt it. A sharp pain in my chest as if somebody had stabbed me in the heart and was twisting away.

The Knife.

At least, this is what I would come to call it. I didn't know it then, but the Knife would become a large part of my life in the coming years. It would become so much a part of me that I wouldn't feel normal without it.

But all I knew about it at this point was that it hurt. A lot. I couldn't understand why Jenn had rejected me. Up until this point, I'd never questioned if there was something wrong with me. But now every possibility supporting that idea was hurtling toward me like fire from a flamethrower. Was I a nerd? Was I ugly? My mind was buried under the weight of these questions as reality began to seep its way into my perception of the Truth.

Sure, I got good grades. I had a brain that seemed to function at a higher level than most of my peers. But did that make me a nerd? Was it the fact that I enjoyed science fiction and superhero comics? That I idolized superheroes like Superman? Shit. Maybe I was a nerd.

What makes a guy ugly, though? I looked into a nearby mirror and began studying my face. I think it was the first time I had ever taken a good look at myself. My face wasn't out of proportion. I didn't have any disgusting deformities. On the other hand, my skin was quite fair, so I didn't exactly fit that whole "tall, dark, and handsome" thing. But did that mean I was ugly?

Maybe I wasn't the best-looking guy around, but I couldn't be downright ugly, could I? My head was swimming with uncertainty and a longing for immediate answers to these questions.

If I had to pinpoint the exact moment I lost my childhood innocence, this was it.

But I wasn't ready to let it go. I wasn't ready to accept this reality, this Truth, just yet. So in the following weeks, I embarked on a quest of sorts. I made a list—a list of girls I was going to ask out. To this day, I am not sure how I summoned the courage to do so, but I asked out twenty-four of the twenty-five girls on the list. The process was different every time; sometimes it was over the phone, sometimes in person. The words I used varied as well. Even their reactions varied, but the results were always the same.

No.

And the Knife would twist away.

I decided not to ask out the last girl on the list. That way, not every girl on the list had told me no. The rejection couldn't be absolute. I could leave a little room for hope.

But that didn't stop the Knife from twisting. It didn't ward off the decimation of my innocence or the invasion of reality into my new Truth.

I was ugly.

I was a nerd.

I was unattractive and undesirable.

I was all of it.

Longing for Belonging

"Wait, let me get this straight...You tried to kill yourself because you were a geek as a kid?

I can hear anger in his voice. I guess I kind of expected this.

"I'm mean, what the fuck? That was years ago. You're not a geek anymore. You seem to do just fine with girls now."

"You are misunderstanding what I'm saying."

"What are you saying?"

"I was simply telling you how it started. The beginning of the story. How the Knife led to curiosity about the idea of suicide, which led to me exploring the possibility. It was a domino effect, and I am just telling you about the first domino. The Knife. A lot more dominos fell that I haven't told you about yet."

He shakes his head in confusion and frustration, his head lowering toward the ground with every shake. In a weird way, I'm happy he has reacted like this. At least he's not pitying me. I don't want pity. I don't want sympathy.

As this goes through my head, a funny thing happens. Like he's heard my thoughts, he asks, "Do you want pity or something?"

I never understood why people felt the need to feel sorry for people in my situation. Pity is the last thing we need. I'll admit, I've personally been guilty of not fully understanding how to deal with a suicidal person. But thinking pity or sympathy could ever possibly help is a ridiculous notion to me. It's like pouring gasoline on a fucking fire.

"That's the last thing I want."

"Then what do you want?"

I crack a smile. What does anybody want? What we want changes constantly, for most of us. Especially when we are young. One minute we want to be an astronaut. The next, a firefighter. And what people want varies from one person to the next. There are some desires that seem universal among human beings, however—primal desires that might be closer to needs than to wants. And they show through from our fears. Our fears are nothing more than the daunting possibility of losing our deepest and most basic desires. The more we fear losing something, the more it can be said that we cherish it.

"Have you ever heard about the claim that people fear public speaking more than Death?"

"Sure."

"Why do you think that is?"

"I don't know. It might not even be true. Could just be some urban myth or something."

"Agreed, but regardless of how accurate it is, public speaking is a huge fear for a lot of people."

"I can agree with that."

"And the reason stems from human nature. Public speaking can threaten one of our most basic and primal desires."

"Sex?" Adam laughs. I let out an empty chuckle.

"Sort of, not really. We have a basic primal need to fit into society. The evolutionary theory of psychology would say it's because we are essentially pack animals and desire a feeling of normality that only comes from being connected in some way to other members of our species. To have a place in society. But if people were to engage in public speaking and make fools of themselves, they risk becoming outcasts, pariahs. They risk not belonging."

Adam gives me an uncertain look before he offers up another challenge.

"Not everybody wants to fit in. What about nonconformists? Those Goth kids in high school and whatnot?"

"I'm not talking about being popular and liked by everyone. You just need to feel like you have a place in this world. We need to feel connected to other people to feel normal. That connection can take many forms. And it can be the smallest group of people that accept you, just as long as somebody accepts you. Nonconformists fit in with other nonconformists. They have a place. They connect. They belong."

"Okay, what about hermits and lone wolves?"

"There are exceptions to every rule, especially when it comes to human beings. However, when you think about it, in a weird way, they do belong. They have a place in the world that they might have even chosen. It feels normal to them. Often people choose to cut off ties to society. I didn't choose to be an outcast, a nerd. I didn't choose to be ugly, to be unwanted."

"So you wanted to be popular?"

"Not exactly."

"Then what?"

"I really just wanted people to like me. Or at least not dislike me. But more than that, I felt the place I wanted to choose for myself in the world being threatened. I was on the verge of manhood. As males, we are all taught at a young age what it is to be a man. It can vary a bit, but I already had an image of what a man is supposed to be. A man is strong. A man doesn't cry. A man attracts women. A man has a family. A man takes care of and protects that family. Nerds and geeks are inherently weak. How could a weak man protect anybody? How could an ugly man attract a woman? The revelation that I repulsed the opposite sex was another emasculating shot to the very core of me. In my mind, it threatened my chances of ever becoming a man. And I wanted to become a man like I was taught to be. But even more than that, even though I knew it was completely ludicrous and not even remotely possible, I wanted to be a superhero. Like Superman. He was the epitome of what it means to be a man. I wanted to be strong enough to protect everyone that couldn't protect themselves— especially those I cared about."

"But you were twelve years old. You weren't a man yet. You weren't even close. And your naïveté is apparent in the fact that you wanted to actually be Superman."

"At that age, everything is final. We are all trying to figure out who we are. And because of that, we tend to be very open to suggestion. When our peers feed us information about who we are during adolescence, we tend to believe them. And when I found out what my peers really thought of me, I was devastated."

"I guess I can agree with you that adolescents often overreact. But didn't you realize that later? Didn't you grow out of it?

"Yes and no."

"What do you mean by that?"

"Yes, I later redefined myself and realized I shouldn't let others dictate my Truth. No, I never really rose above what is sometimes referred to as 'precarious manhood.' Manhood, in our society, is considered something that one must continually earn. We must constantly prove our manhood. It's something I still struggle with."

Adam nods. "I can relate to that."

"I would bet that all men can, at least to some degree. The idea of precarious manhood also made it quite difficult for me to get out of the way of the falling dominos."

"So what other dominos fell?"

"There were a lot of them. But we aren't quite there yet. And all of this talk about needs has reminded me of another primal need." I grab the pole supporting my IV bag and slowly attempt to maneuver my legs so that they hang over the side of the bed. "I need to take a piss."

"Wait, I don't think that is a good idea."

"I'm not pissing in a fucking bedpan. My liver might be failing, but my legs are working just fine."

Wrong. My legs are shaking so badly that it takes several attempts to finally stand, making me feel like an idiot for my previous statement. Pride, however, invigorates me, and I manage to stand up using the IV pole as an improvised cane. I remember seeing the bathroom on the way in. Lucky for me, it is right outside of my door. Walking across the hall, I get some puzzled looks from nurses and orderlies passing by, but none of them says word one to me. Maybe they're too busy to say anything. Maybe I don't look as awkward as I feel like I do. Maybe they just don't give a shit. Who knows? Who cares?

I make it through the bathroom doorway and use the wall of the bathroom as additional support. Urinating isn't the hard part. The hospital gown doesn't require much effort to get out of the way. The hard part is trying to wash my hands while supporting myself on the IV pole well enough to not fall over. The wall is too far from the sink to lean on for support, as I did while I urinated. Fuck it. I'm not really worried about germs at this point. A quick splash of water on each hand will have to do.

My trek back across the hall feels a little easier and quicker, probably because I don't have to try so hard not to piss myself as I walk.

"You really shouldn't be walking." I hear the voice as I'm struggling to get back into the bed. It's not

Adam, but a female voice coming from my door. The nurse that installed my IV walks into the room carrying a large jug of brown liquid. I must have been super out of it when they rolled me in here, because even though I remember her, I barely recognize her. And I normally notice attractive women. She's older than me, late twenties, possibly early thirties—blond hair, brown eyes, and as I said, a very striking woman.

"Great, the booze is here. Let's get this party started."

"Not booze," she replies. "Better."

"Well, there's only one liquid I can think of that's better than booze, and a gallon is a shitload of LSD."

"Apple juice."

"Oh, goodie."

"And not just any apple juice. This is special apple juice. It's going to help clean out your system."

"And make me piss like a racehorse?"

"Exactly."

Great. The treacherous journey to the bathroom will have to be repeated several times again.

She shoots me a fake smile and sets the jug on the rolling table by my bed, along with a little paper cup.

"Drink up."

With that, she walks out of the room. I unscrew the lid with my hands still shaking and attempt to pour some into the cup. I tip the jug too much, and the liquid knocks over the flimsy paper cup and spills onto the table and floor.

"Fuck me!" I yell as I plunk the jug back down.

Adam chimes in, "You want me to help you?"

"Fuck it. I'll drink it straight from the jug."

I rest the jug on my chest and use my stomach muscles in conjunction with my hands to tilt the jug up to my mouth just enough to slurp a small bit out. I cringe.

"It tastes like apple-flavored cough syrup. Mixed with dog shit."

"Drink it—it's good for you."

"Yeah, yeah."

I take another sip of the apple drink and lean back onto the bed. It really isn't all that bad tasting. It pretty much just tastes like apple juice. I guess I just feel like complaining. I hate this feeling. I feel so helpless. I feel so weak. I feel so...

Worthless.

"Aren't you scared?"

"Of what? Dying?"

"Yeah, I mean, you're acting like nothing is wrong. As if everything is normal, like nothing is different from the same old, same old."

"Nothing is different from the same old, same old. I haven't really expected to live past my twenty-first birthday for a long time now."

"But it's human nature to fear Death."

"It's animal nature to fear Death. All living beings have an innate desire for survival. Yet humans are the only species that intentionally end their own lives, the only species that kill for reasons other than necessity. And nobody really knows why. It's amazing, with all our advancements in technology, all of the knowledge we have amassed over these last few thousand years, the one subject we really know almost nothing about is ourselves."

"We know a lot about ourselves. What about psychology?"

I can't help but scoff. My disdain for the medical field in general isn't nearly as extensive as my contempt for the field of psychology. "What a joke."

"What do you mean?" Adam asks, a look of genuine puzzlement on his face.

"The medical profession, and more specifically the field of psychology, has essentially been bought out by the big pharmaceutical companies—both in terms of the way medicine is practiced and how it's researched. Much of the so called 'research' being carried out is categorically false."

"You aren't one of those idiots that doesn't believe mental illness exists, are you?" Adam's look of puzzlement changes to one of contempt.

"No. But it is completely misunderstood and extremely overdiagnosed."

"They've proven that depression is a chemical imbalance."

"They haven't proven shit. The chemical-imbalance theory is an archaic idea from the 1950s. The only reason it is still perpetuated is that it is easily monetized by Big Pharma in the form of antidepressants. Antidepressants are the most commonly prescribed drugs in North America. They are the bread and butter of Big Pharma."

"But antidepressants work. They help a lot of people," Adam's look of contempt softens a bit.

"They may help some people, but whether they work is debatable. Just because mood can be manipulated by drugs doesn't prove the chemical-imbalance theory is correct. About a third of people that take them aren't helped at all by them. And there is no way to know how many of the other two-thirds are experiencing benefits from the placebo effect. It has been proven that we can effectively rewire our brains. So it's quite possible that many people improve simply because they think the pills are helping them and rewire their own brains as such."

"How do you know this? I mean, I think doctors and researchers would know better than you. No offense."

"Many of them do know this. And that's where I get my information from—independent studies carried out without the bias of Big Pharma funding. For example, a study done in the seventies where researchers massively increased the serotonin levels in severely depressed patients and found that it had no effect whatsoever on their depression levels. Some in the medical profession that know, however, don't care. There is just too much money involved to rock the boat. Capitalism has many benefits, but one downfall is that sometimes that which is best for society isn't pursued simply because it isn't profitable. The perpetuation of ignorance and misinformation is encouraged if it helps to sell something."

"I'm having a hard time believing that. You sound like some crazy conspiracy theorist," Although Adam's look of contempt has softened, it's still there.

"It's the same with ADHD. Ritalin and Adderall are essentially just legal speed. They have very similar effects as cocaine. Adderall is almost identical to crystal meth, chemically speaking. They amp up your nervous system. They will make anybody focus better, regardless of ADHD or not."

Adam shakes his head. "I have close friends that really do have ADHD."

"I'm not saying that it doesn't exist, even though a founding father of ADHD proclaimed it to be a 'fictitious disease.' But there is no doubt that it's extremely overdiagnosed. And just maybe, providing speed to kids isn't the best way to treat it. But it's the treatment that is most easily monetized, so it's the one they sell us."

"I guess now that you mention it, I do know a lot of people that have been prescribed Adderall that probably don't have ADHD. So if pills aren't the answer, what is?"

"I don't know. I didn't say pills aren't the answer—I was just pointing out why pills are always offered as the only answer. Money."

"Are you saying depression is s fictitious disease too?"

"No. I wouldn't call it a disease at all."

Adam scoffs. "Of course it's a disease."

"A disease is an attack by external source, not something we do to ourselves—not something that is in our nature. Depression is no more a disease than addiction is."

"Oh, here we go. You *are* one of those people that don't believe in mental illness, aren't you?"

"No. There are many mental illnesses. It's just that depression isn't one of them. The only reason people think that way is because, again, Big Pharma has convinced them it's a disease so they can sell them pills. Being depressed is an emotional state. If being depressed is a disease, then so is happiness."

"But happiness is good. Depression isn't."

"It doesn't have to be a disease in order to cause suffering."

"Okay. For argument's sake, let's say it isn't a disease. What is it then?"

I smirk. "I don't think you are ready to hear it yet. You still haven't accepted what depression isn't."

"You are kind of an asshole—you know that?"

I chuckle. "I've been told that before."

"I think I have a good idea of what depression is. I'm not stupid. It's extreme sadness."

"Wrong again. Depression isn't really sadness."

"You lost me again."

"Let's move on to the next domino. Maybe that will clear some things up."

"If you say so."

Be a Man

I felt like crying. I tried to cry. This was one instance it would be acceptable for a man to cry. I just couldn't. I felt the sadness. Yet, the idea that a man doesn't cry had been so ingrained into me at this point that I couldn't cry at my grandmother's funeral.

I had just turned thirteen, the summer before eighth grade. She had been diagnosed with lung cancer a few years prior but had gone into remission. However, not too long ago, it came back and spread to her brain.

She had come to stay with us in between the two cancer diagnoses. Obviously, we didn't know the second one was imminent. We thought she had beaten it.

I don't remember how long exactly she stayed, probably a few months, but it wasn't long enough for me. Despite the fact that she had more than thirty grandchildren other than me, and despite that she lived two thousand miles away, we had always been fairly close. And we had grown even closer during her stay.

I had asked her once why she always helped me with my chores when she didn't seem to do that with anyone else. She replied, "So we can get to playing Scrabble."

We played a lot of Scrabble. We played a lot of card games too—poker, go fish, et cetera. Grandma loved games. So did I. Needless to say, we played all different types of games, but they always required at least some level of mental acuity. I don't remember us ever playing anything that was a complete game of chance. Maybe that's why we got along so well.

Grandma was pretty smart, so maybe we just enjoyed challenging each other's minds.

It might be sad to say, but she was probably my best friend at the time. Don't get me wrong—I had friends. Just not any good ones. My friendship with Ethan was still new. Hanging out with anyone outside of school or sports was an extremely rare occurrence. And it always seemed as though I was the one to extend the invitation, never the other way around. In fact, I don't really remember getting invited to anything by anyone.

So there I was, a young boy in the midst of adolescence. No real friends to speak of. No girlfriend, obviously. A brain that seemed to work better than my peers', as evidenced by my straight-A grades. An interest in sci-fi and superheroes. And my only real friend was my grandmother.

I was the epitome of a nerd.

And a prime target for a bully.

Almost.

Bullies like easy targets. Their goal, even if they don't really understand it, is to lift themselves up by putting others down. Or, "They want to knock someone's head off so they look taller," as I've heard it described. The easier it is to put someone else down, the better. And since I had already accepted that I was a nerd as Truth, I must have seemed like I was one of those easy targets—at least, to this one kid named Brent.

By the eighth grade, I had pretty much given up. I still liked girls and continued developing crushes even though I knew they didn't like me back. I wish could have just turned that part of myself off. But the confidence derived from the resolve to prove I wasn't a nerd had disappeared. I had retreated into myself and developed a shyness that emanated from me like a visible glowing aura. I might as well have simply worn a sign that read, PLEASE PICK ON ME.

Brent and I were both on the basketball team. I guess technically we weren't on the same team. He was on the "A" team, the junior high school equivalent of the varsity team. I was on the "C" team. That's where they put all of the kids they would have just cut, but they had one of those policies that if you wanted to play, you were on the team. Nobody got cut.

I wasn't a terrible basketball player per se. I led all three teams in steals. I was good at reading the opposing players and predicting when and where they were going to move the ball to, either via a pass to another player or a juke move while dribbling. Shooting the ball and coming anywhere near the basket, however, was a completely different story.

I could make baskets just fine in practice, especially when nobody was looking. But I would just get so nervous in a game with everyone watching me that I would usually do the exact thing that I was afraid of. The clear majority of the very few shots I took in games didn't even hit the backboard. A couple sailed right over the top. The ones that did hit that backboard were usually thrown way too hard and would bounce back several feet to be picked up by the opposing team in a spectacularly embarrassing fashion.

Even though I had finally started to make some friends on the team, overall, I just wanted to quit. But a man doesn't quit. A man finishes what he starts. So I stuck it out through the season, taking a small comfort in the fact that it would soon be over, and I wouldn't have to play again in high school. I wouldn't have to quit—I just wouldn't go out for the team. Had it not been for Brent, though, I might have reconsidered trying to play again in high school.

Brent had a problem that made him act out the way he did. Even though he was very athletic, he was rather…short. I hadn't even hit my big growth spurt yet, and I towered a good six inches over him. Maybe that's another reason why he targeted me. The only thing a man is probably more self-conscious about than the length of his body is the length of a body part unique to the male gender. I think you know which one I'm talking about. The quintessential ideal man is tall, dark, and handsome, after all. At least I've always had one of those going for me. I wasn't the tallest on the team by any means, but I was probably the tallest nerd. Maybe that's another reason why Brent targeted me.

I don't remember what prompted him to start in on me. Maybe I had tried to tell a joke that just didn't come out very funny. Even though I had accepted that I was a nerd as Truth, I still had a burning desire to change it. One of the ways I attempted that feat was to work extensively on my sense of humor. People like people that are funny. If I were thought of as the class clown, it would be a far cry from nerd.

I know now that many—possibly most, if not all—comedians start off and probably continually use their humor as a defense mechanism.

I was successful at least to some extent. But as with any endeavor to redefine oneself, there were setbacks. As any wannabe funny person will tell you, it's damn near impossible to be funny all the time. Bad jokes that invoke no laughter are inevitable.

Perhaps I had attempted one of these ill-fated jokes just prior to the onslaught of social torture Brent unleashed upon me. Perhaps I didn't. Perhaps I was just there. Again, I don't really remember.

What I do remember, however, is everything he did to me and called me in those few months. It all happened in the locker room, away from the prying eyes of coaches or any adults at all.

It started out with name-calling, as I imagine is the norm. "Nerd." "Fag." "Retard." All the usual suspects. It gradually escalated from there. The first instance of escalation, he took my shoes and threw them into the toilet. According to Brent, since they weren't an expensive name brand like Nike Air Jordans, costing $150, they were a "retard's shoes." I'm pretty sure my mother had purchased them at either a thrifty secondhand clothing store or a large discount retailer such as Costco; the two provided the bulk of all my and my siblings' clothing. Objectively speaking, they were actually very nice shoes. My mother did a very good job of finding nice clothes at a discount, and we were all dressed quite well.

After all, my family wasn't genuinely poor. In fact, many people thought we were quite well off because we lived in a rather large house, at least in comparison to others in the area. But we were also a rather large family, at least in comparison to others in the area. In a family with four kids, thrift spending, at least to some extent, is basically required. My siblings were my older brother by three years, Evan; my younger brother by two years, Danny; and my little sister by four years, Isabella, or Bella, as we called her. We had adopted her when she was two because my mother had wanted a daughter and didn't want to risk having another boy.

And what most people didn't realize, along with everyone in my family, save my father, was that a large amount of debt was accruing to support our large family—even with my mother's thrift shopping. A debt that would become so massive, our family would eventually be crushed under the weight of it. Of course, it wasn't the real reason for the devastation to come, but it would pile on top of and contribute to the main reason.

As a result of our large house and nice clothes that weren't the same ridiculously overpriced clothes the "cool kids" wore, I was ironically made fun of for being rich and poor at same time. Yet the name-calling, the submerging of my shoes in toilet water—I let all that slide. I didn't retaliate in any way. I would just remain silent. I would simply retrieve my shoes and hang them up in my locker to dry without a single word. I figured that if I didn't show that he was getting to me, he would stop.

But he never did.

In fact, he got worse. Everybody has their breaking point. A last straw. Up until this point, I had been adhering to the old "Sticks and stones may break my bones, but words will never hurt me" adage. Okay, that's misleading. I really hadn't retaliated verbally or otherwise because I still just wanted everyone to like me, even this asshole. I'm still not even sure why it meant so much to me. Perhaps that ingrained need to belong?

Either way, the feeling was trumped when Brent decided to up the stakes by slamming my fingers in my locker door. I saw red as my inner machismo took over, and I instinctually threw a punch. It landed squarely on his sternum and knocked him back a few steps. If I had caught him on the jaw, I have no doubt he would have dropped like a sack of potatoes. I still wonder if I subconsciously avoided nailing him in the face because of this reason. It might have been that I simply overcompensated for his height—or rather, the lack thereof.

The red didn't stick around long. The tears welling up in his eyes cleared that red right out of mine. I could tell he'd realized he had just made a grave error. He attempted to save face and made a half-assed move as if to return fire. All it took was for me to raise my fist slightly as if about to launch another one at him, and he backed right off again. He resolved himself to saving face by calling me names as he slowly backed up.

I don't remember what he said. I didn't care. A surprising feeling had come over me—pity. When I saw his tears begin to well up, I felt sorry for him. I felt bad for hitting him.

It wasn't the first time I'd felt bad after something like that. Three years prior, while I was walking home from school, another bully by the name of Dustin had decided I was a good target too. He was also most likely suffering from an acute case of Napoleon Syndrome and no doubt thought I would be an easy victim as well. But he didn't escalate things gradually.

He was yelling insults as he walked toward me. When he got to me, he took a swing—a swing and a miss. It happened rather quickly, and I don't remember exactly how I did it, but I took him down to the ground and was on top of him, pummeling him in his face. After several blows to his head, I asked him, "Are you done?"

He nodded. I let him up, and I walked off. I didn't look back. He didn't say a word as I left. I saw him the next day with a bruise on his cheek.

Both Dustin and Brent, a few years later, acted the same way in the aftermath. They avoided even making eye contact with me. I felt bad for them.

I didn't like hurting other people. This probably originated in my desire for people to like me, which originated in my primal need to belong. But just because I didn't enjoy fighting, didn't mean I wasn't good at it. It might have had something to do with growing up with two brothers and the experiences of fighting with them. But I think the primary culprit was something else. What neither of those bullies knew was that I had already been dealing with the ultimate bully my entire life. He was the supreme emperor of Bullydom.

My father.

I've been talking about the idea of what it is to be a man. We all develop this idea from different sources.

We get notions from television and advertising. We take cues from society and our peers. But the comprehensive picture I developed, the vast majority of this idea, came from my father.

He wasn't a very physically imposing man, maybe five feet nine and 170 pounds with a beer gut. He had a mustache, he often wore a fanny pack and dorky glasses, and he would perm his hair. An archetypal nerd. The concept of "like father, like son" probably only reinforced my acceptance of myself as one too.

Yet underneath a seemingly innocuous exterior, a powder keg of rage was lying in wait for the most trivial irritant to ignite it. The phrase "bad temper" doesn't even come close to describing it. It didn't take much to set him off, and once unleashed, his booming voice would spray terror-inducing anger into the air. Anyone in close proximity would be affected by it. Surrounded by it. Permeated by it.

The volume of his voice wasn't the sole contributing factor to his claim to the title of superlative oppressor. The specific words he would use inflicted comparable damage. Mainly, he seemed content with barking orders like some overacting drill sergeant from the movies. But he also liked to occasionally pepper his shouting tantrums with insults, mostly attacks on our intelligence. He was quite fond of asking, "Are you stupid or something?" Not the sort of thing any child is too excited to hear coming from his or her father.

While shouting was commonplace, my father rarely became physically violent. Nonetheless, there were a few noteworthy incidents.

The one I remember the best happened while driving in the mountains. I had cousins visiting from out of state, and my dad wanted to show them the natural beauty of Colorado. I can't remember how old I was exactly, but I was probably around ten. Right around the time of the fight with Dustin.

I was fine for the first few hours. Maybe it was something I ate. Maybe it was all the jostling from hitting the bumps and dips on the dirt roads we had been driving down. Maybe it was both. Regardless, I started to feel sick to my stomach.

When I informed my father, he told me something to the effect of, "Grow a pair." I tried to tough it out. I maybe lasted another hour before I couldn't take it any longer. By that point, the pain had traveled to every corner of my body, and I just felt awful all over.

"Just let me out."

"What?"

"Just let me out—pick me up on the way back."

"I'm not doing that."

"Why not? It's not like anything is going to happen to me. I'm just going to lie down in the grass."

"Stop being such a wimp."

"It hurts!"

He slammed on the brakes. "Fine, get out. But I'm not picking you back up. Just walk your happy ass home."

"Fine with me."

My mother was pleading with my father to reconsider as I exited the truck. My cousins were wearing concerned looks on their faces. He drove off as soon as I closed the door.

I began walking even though I knew it was way too far to walk back home. We had been driving for hours and were close to the top of a mountain, several miles away from any hint of civilization and dozens of miles away from our house. But I didn't care. I was already starting to feel infinitely better, not being bounced about from the shifting of the truck to conform to the road.

I didn't get very far before I heard the creaking of the shocks and whir of the engine coming back toward me. I just kept walking.

"Get in the truck."

"Are we going home?"

"No."

"I'm good." I turned and continued walking.

"Get in the truck now!"

"No."

You could feel it in the air. He was about to explode. I expected a fury of shouts and insults, but I guess I pissed him off something extra this time. He stomped toward me, and as soon as I turned around, he kicked me right in my stomach. I dropped to the ground before the holler of pain finished exiting my lungs.

I could hear muffled voices around me as I writhed in pain on the ground, the tears forming in the corners of my eyes. I couldn't quite make out what was being said, but I'm sure it was my mother pleading with my father to stop.

When the pain started to subside and things began to clear up a bit, I slowly rose to my feet. He had taken a few steps back, and my mother was still in full-on beseeching mode next to him. Perhaps it was a newfound confidence from the fight with Dustin. Perhaps my precarious manhood was just starting to kick into high gear. Whatever it was, a sheen of insolence was radiating from me even through the tears streaming down my face as I exclaimed: "FUCK YOU!"

"What did you just say to me?"

"FUCK Y—"

I couldn't get the second proclamation of defiance out before he kicked me again as my mother futilely attempted to hold him back. This one landed a little higher and knocked the wind out of me. I squirmed and wheezed on the ground for an indiscernible length of time. When I finally caught my breath, the tears were gushing. This time, my mother helped me to my feet.

I took stock of my surroundings; my father was sitting behind the wheel of the truck, a scowl on his face. The truck was empty other than that. The other previous occupants had exited at some point and were gathered around me now.

"Come on. Let's go," my mother said as she led me back to the truck. "Don't even look at him. Just get in." With that, my mother spoke the last words anybody would speak for the rest of the trip. Nobody said a single word until we got back to our house. I just dried my eyes and stared out the window. My stomach still hurt, but the pain seemed inconsequential to the anger boiling inside me.

It was an anger I had no doubt inherited from him. A father is supposed to be a model for his sons to strive toward. And honestly, for the most part, he was an example of a good father. Empirically speaking, anyway. He always showed up to our sporting events and extracurricular activities. He taught us a lot of valuable life lessons and gave good advice.

During his rampages, however, he was a never-ending, prime example of what not to do. I didn't want to be like him at all. Yet he still inadvertently taught me many things in those moments too—notably, the importance of being a strong, powerful man. And how, despite a popular but incorrect axiom to the contrary, violence can in fact solve problems. Anybody that tells you differently is out of touch with reality.

My father would kick me once more a few years after the encounter on the mountain. Evidently, he was fond of kicking. I can't remember the exact circumstances, but I'm sure I was being a defiant smartass on this occasion too. The setting had changed—it was in the kitchen at our home. But this time was different than before. The kick only knocked me a step back and did not drop me to the floor. And there was no second kick. I stood my ground, and he backed off. And I didn't tear up.

A little after that was the Brent incident, another example of how violence can solve problems. Neither Brent nor Dustin ever attempted to bully me again. And finally, after I hit my growth spurt and grew about seven inches the summer between junior high and high school, my father tried one last time.

Again, I can't remember how I set him off that time, but when he started to lift his leg for his signature kick, I kicked his shin back down. Immediately he threw a punch. I'm not sure how or why my reaction was what it was. I dodged the punch, grabbed his arm, and used his forward momentum against him to do what is called a hip throw. In one fluid motion, my father was lying on his back, looking up. The look of absolute astonishment on his face told me that he knew. He knew he couldn't push me around anymore.

That's not to say he instantly changed his ways. He was still a complete asshole with a meteoric temper and a thundering roar. But he never laid a finger on me again.

Looking down at his stunned expression, I felt as if I had earned my manhood. I felt strong. I felt powerful. I was a man—a man that had conquered his tormenter.

But looking down at my grandmother, lying in her coffin, I didn't feel like a man. I felt tremendously sad.

But I couldn't cry, no matter how much I felt like it. Was this what it meant to be a man? Wasn't a man allowed to cry, or at least tear up, in situations like these? Or did a real man never cry? Had I become a man? Did the fact that I couldn't cry mean I had shed my boyhood innocence?

I never did answer those questions. But the fact remained.

When my grandmother died, I couldn't cry.

A Comparison of Misery

Adam shakes his head.

"You're acting like your life was so rough. Sure, your dad was an asshole. But there are so many people that have had worse fathers. Way worse. You said yourself that he rarely was physically violent. There are people that get beaten by their fathers on a daily basis."

"And I said that overall he was actually a pretty good father. But again, you are missing the point."

"What's the point then?"

"What is it that you really want to say to me right now? Aren't you really trying to tell me that I'm being a pussy?"

Adam straightens up in his chair. "Yeah. You are."

"I appreciate your honesty. But therein lies the point. That is your own precarious manhood taking over. You see a man not 'being a man' and feel the urge to call him out on it. And that is the whole point. I wanted to demonstrate what precarious manhood is and how it governs so many of our thoughts and actions."

"So you aren't trying to compare your life to others and say it has been bad?" Adam leans back in his chair a bit, taking a less confrontational posture.

"Not even a little bit. My life hasn't been all that bad, relatively speaking. But it has something in common with so-called 'bad lives.' There is this misconception that people become depressed because their lives are bad—and a fallacy that people that commit suicide are selfish cowards. That they can't handle the pain, so they take the easy way out."

"But isn't there some Truth to that? I always thought that people don't kill themselves because they want to die, but they are just trying to make the pain stop," Adam's confrontational posture all but disappears, suggesting he is authentically trying to understand.

"First, there's nothing easy about suicide. Second, by the time a person gets to the point of committing suicide, something inside has fundamentally changed. When asking why and looking for the cause, people are always looking too far ahead in the process. The answer can't be found there. We have to look back to the beginning."

"But isn't that what we've been doing? Looking at the beginning? And I'm just as confused, if not more so than before we started."

"It's pointless to compare one person's life to another's and try to determine who is worse off. For one thing, it's subjective. People have varying definitions of what is good and what is bad. Different Truths. And more than that, it's not an indicator of depression. How else would you explain people that seemingly have horrible lives, yet they are the happiest people you could ever meet? Or on the other side of the coin, how do you explain people that seemingly have wonderful lives, but for some reason are depressed?"

"So what's the connection? What do they have in common?" he asks.

"There's the right question. I knew you had it in you," I reply as a smirk forms on my face.

"There you go being a condescending asshole again," Adam scoffs.

"I try."

"So what is it?"

"You tell me."

"I don't know. That's why I am asking you, dick." Adam is starting to look frustrated again.

"Just think on it for a minute. What have I been talking about? What didn't I have when I realized I was a nerd? What did I lack when I was being bullied?"

You can almost hear the gears turning in his head. "Control?"

"Bingo. A feeling of control. No choice. I didn't choose to be a nerd, but that is how I was labeled. I couldn't stop my bullies, at least not without violence. But more than that, I wasn't able to control that need for belonging. I had no say in my place in the world. And I think for a lot of people, this feeling of helplessness is what leads to the first thoughts of suicide. Because even if you have no command over anything, you still have the option to end your own life. And just thinking about it makes you feel like you are taking some of that control back."

"For a lot of people? I thought we were talking about what they all have in common. What causes them all to be so sad they want to kill themselves?"

"There are a few things wrong with that question. First, everybody is different. This is why it's so hard for psychology to come up with hard-set rules for human behavior. We all see the world differently and react differently to stimuli. We all have our own distinctive Truths. Secondly, depression is not the only path to suicide. It's probably the most common, but they are not necessarily tantamount to each other. Finally, 'sadness' and 'depression' are not synonymous. I was sad when my grandmother died. I was not depressed."

"What do you mean? By definition, depression is extreme sadness. We can look it up in the dictionary if you want to."

"Depression is emptiness, not sadness."

Somehow, that statement seems to resonate with Adam. He nods. "You know, that makes a lot of sense."

"We get a sense of fulfillment from satisfying our primal needs. When we don't, there's a hole, an emptiness inside us that we try to fill by any other means we can. Sometimes we accept Truths we don't choose or want. Sometimes we try to fill the hole with alcohol or drugs. But nothing can fill that hole like having genuine connections to other people. There have been several studies that show people develop addictions not because the substances themselves are addicting and the addicts enjoy them more, but because they lack those genuine connections. They don't have that sense of belonging and are making a futile attempt to fill the gaping crater in their lives."

"And you are saying this is why depression and addiction are connected?"

"I would say they are more than connected. Both arise from the same desolation. Both stem from attempts to become whole again, to feel normal. We all want to feel a sense of normalcy."

I realize I should probably pause there. I don't think Adam is quite ready to accept where it is heading.

As I am contemplating which direction I should veer the conversation to, Adam changes the direction for me. "So you accepted your Truth as a nerd in an attempt to fill the emptiness. And when that didn't work?"

"I turned to something else. Something that is good at tricking people into thinking it is working. And in some regards, it does. But usually, it just complicates things."

The Booze That Soothes

It seemed like a good idea at the time. I guess I'm just lucky it was a pink highlighter and not a permanent marker that just happened to be sitting there. Considering the state I was in, a permanent marker probably would have seemed like a good idea too. Just about anything that popped into my mind would probably have seemed like a good idea.

For some still-unknown reason, I grabbed that highlighter and began drawing a happy face…on my own face. Well, not a completely unknown reason. It obviously had something do with the fact that I had just become drunk for the first time in my life—at least, the first time I can remember.

Apparently when I was two years old, my great-uncle gave me a beer, unbeknownst to my parents. And I drank the whole thing. Or so I have been told. I imagine that even just one beer would have had quite the intoxicating effect on a two-year-old. But I have no memory of it at all, so I can't confirm it.

Fast-forward ten years. Switch out my great-uncle for my older brother and his friends thinking it would be funny to get Evan's little brother drunk. After drinking four of what I can only assume were fruit-punch-flavored wine coolers, I'm drawing smiley faces on my own face with a pink highlighter.

One might think the next day I would have felt some modicum of embarrassment, but I didn't. I had been shown a whole new world, a world where I felt in control, even though it was an illusion. And I liked it. I liked it a lot.

Sure, I liked drinking alcohol for the typical reasons. It made me feel good. Everything was more interesting. Music sounded better. Everyone was more attractive. Any trace of shyness fell away. It was just fun.

But my favorite aspect was that my give-a-fuck meter would drop to zero. I just didn't care what anybody thought of me. Being thought of as a nerd didn't bother me. Girls not liking me didn't faze me at all. I felt free. Free of the need to belong. Free of the fear of not earning my manhood. Of being alone. It soothed the pain from the Knife. It was the perfect remedy, albeit a temporary one, for my problems.

I just didn't give a flying fuck.

So after that first time, I began thinking of ways to do it again. Siphoning wine from the box my mother kept in the fridge. Taking a beer here and a beer there from my father's cases in the fridge and hiding them.

Drinking them when I felt I had saved up enough of them for a proper buzz. Replacing booze in my parents' liquor cabinet with water. On one occasion, I even took an entire bottle of brandy. I had never seen them drinking brandy, so I didn't think they would notice it was missing. And they didn't.

Don't get me wrong. I didn't instantly become the raging alcoholic you know today. I wasn't drinking all the time. I wouldn't even say it was all that frequent—at least, not at this point.

By the second half of eighth grade, things had started to look up for me. I had started to make real friends, friends that invited me to hang out and do fun things, like go to the Lodge together. Three friends, to be exact: Ethan, who I mentioned; Jason, or Jay, as we tended to call him, who was the son of my mother's best friend; and Desmond, or Dez, who had recently moved to the area. To be fair, Dez might have come a little later, perhaps freshman year, but the exact timeline is hard to nail down.

Our friendship began on the basketball team even though I was the only one on the "C" team. And we kept hanging out after basketball ended. One difference between Ethan and Jay/Dez, however, was that Jay and Dez liked to drink on occasion, like me.

We went to the Lodge together almost every weekend, starting the winter of our last year in junior high school. We would dare each other to ask the girls to dance. And to my utter astonishment, whenever I got up the courage to ask a girl to dance, she would almost inevitable say yes. It was a major confidence booster.

And even more amazing, in February of that year, I finally landed my first official girlfriend. Jessica was very pretty, intelligent, and kindhearted. All of this only added to my bewilderment when one of her friends told me that Jessica liked me.

I remember telling myself to play it cool, but I'm not sure I was able to contain my excitement when I replied that I liked her too. I guess it was my elation that allowed me to overcome my nervousness and go over and talk to her.

I doubt anything was said of consequence that day at her locker. But I do know I couldn't stop smiling the whole time. And she was smiling too! We talked and set up our first date to meet at the Lodge that weekend.

It only lasted a month, but it was the best month of my life at the time. Every day was more exhilarating than the one before. We kissed for the first time on that first date at the Lodge. For the first time ever, I had a valentine on Valentine's Day. We'd pass little innocent love letters back and forth. I don't think I stopped smiling for that entire month.

And even when she told me she didn't want to date anymore, while it hurt, I wasn't devastated. I felt the Knife, but it wasn't all that intense. I know now that I have ignorance to thank for that.

I had thought this had been a sign that things had turned around for me. But I was ignorant to the fact that I wouldn't have a girlfriend again for another five years. Not a single high school sweetheart. I didn't know that I would be alone for every Valentine's Day thereafter—that I would be alone every day.

I learned these facts gradually as time went on. And gradually the frequency and intensity of the Knife increased in direct proportion. In turn, the frequency of my alcohol use also increased.

As I mentioned before, the summer before my freshman year, I hit my big growth spurt. I grew almost seven inches in five months. I damn near reached my current height of about six feet. This also gave me reason to hope; yet in reality, all it did was perpetuate my ignorance. I figured girls would notice me more now. But they didn't.

I did, however, make strides in the friend department. At least it felt like I did. I wish I could say my witty sense of humor and my keen intellect were the main driving forces for this progress, that I somehow transformed into somebody other people wanted to be around. But alcohol, it seemed, wore that badge of honor.

The fact that alcohol was a social lubricant due to its inhibition-disintegration properties helped. Social interactions at least seemed easier when my give-a-fuck disappeared. But that's not really what I mean.

Having an older brother, and knowing some older people through my job at a local grocery store, I had an advantage that most people my age didn't. I had access to alcohol. I could get it with relative ease. And even though I may not have realized it at the time, I think that was the main driving force behind my social success.

Don't get me wrong—I know it wasn't the only reason. After all, Ethan didn't even really drink. But he hung around less and less as time went on. The bulk of my social interactions throughout high school involved alcohol. I was usually the person to procure it for everyone—and not just alcohol. I could also get marijuana. That was easier to get than alcohol as the person selling it was never concerned with checking my ID to verify age. But alcohol tended to be the main focus.

So it stands to reason that many of my so-called friends merely hung around me because I was the unofficial "candy man." I only wished I didn't have to realize the hard way that these friendships were hollow, that I didn't really have a bunch of friends.

I had customers.

A Deadline Approaches

"Come on, man." Adam rolls his eyes. "You can't honestly believe that every person you called a friend only hung around you because you could get them weed or booze. You said yourself that your friend Ethan didn't really even drink."

"Yeah, but I also said he slowly hung out less and less. He played football and started hanging around with other football players more. Jay, D, and I were all on the soccer team. And as a result, we became closer friends. I also threw that disclaimer out there that I know it wasn't the only reason they hung around. I'd had several years to work on my sense of humor and had become fairly decent at making people laugh. But I know if the shit really hit the fan, not a single one of them would be anywhere in sight."

Adam rubs his eyes and exhales heavily. He's got to be getting tired. I'm growing sleepy myself. College kids aren't built to wake up at the crack of dawn.

"Why don't you go home and get some sleep?"

My suggestion perks him up a bit. "I'm fine."

"No, really, it's cool. I'm gonna take a nap myself."

"All right. You need anything?"

I chuckle. As if he could really get me anything I need.   "My contacts would be nice. It somehow slipped my mind to put them in this morning." A weak joke.

"You sure you'll be okay?"

"Yeah, no worries."

"Okay, I'll be back in a bit."

He disappears as my eyes close. The metallic room with no escape tries to take center stage of my dreams again—but I have another dream this time. I dream about the night I bought the pills. It is so real, it's as if I have traveled back in time to that moment.

It is around 11:00 p.m. The store is all but empty. I walk through the automatic doors and past the lady at the solitary open register. The pharmacy is in the back and is slightly darker than the rest of the store as a fluorescent bulb has burned out.

My left hand grasps the box of Tylenol PM, my right, the box of generic store-brand sleeping pills. The two boxes are right next to each other. I flip the boxes over and read the warnings. They say the exact same thing. The Tylenol costs a few dollars more.

I think to myself, "What's a few extra dollars if I'm going to be dead? Might as well spring for the name brand…"

And then I wake up. I look over and see Adam there, a distraught look on his face. It only takes me a second to realize what's happened. "So you asked the doctors to deliver the news yourself?"

Adam's eyebrows furrow.

"I know I'm dying."

"How do you know that?"

"The two boxes I chose between were sitting right next to each other on the shelf at the store. They always do that with stuff that is basically identical. The only difference is the brand and the price. Not to mention that I remember having the thought that it didn't really matter what the price was, and I might as well spend the extra cash and get the name brand, which certainly had Tylenol in it as it was in the friggin' title on the box."

Adam's head drops toward the floor. Neither of us says anything until his head pops back up, and he exclaims, "It's okay. You'll be able to get the transplant, and you'll be just fine."

I pause for a few seconds, thinking of how I should say this. I guess it doesn't really matter how I say it. It's going to piss him off. "I'm not going to get the transplant."

"Don't think like that. Sure you are. The doctor said you have a very good chance of getting a new liver as you are so young and in college and whatnot."

"No. You don't understand. I'm not going to get the transplant."

"What?"

"I'm not going to take a liver away from somebody that needs it through no fault of their own, simply because I'm younger and society deems me more valuable, as a college student, than they are."

"That's bullshit, man. You made a mistake. It happens. But the mistake can be fixed. You have every right at a chance to fix it."

"Will it fix it, though? Sure, I'll probably live. But for how long? A new liver won't stop me from doing this or something similar again."

"Why would you do anything like this ever again? You can get help. You can take antidepressants and get better."

"I've been taking antidepressants for several months now. I've been seeing a therapist at the school. Neither is doing a damn thing. You're still thinking of depression like it's a disease. Something that can be treated or even cured. It's just not that simple."

Adam's teeth grind, and his fists clench.

"Whatever. You're getting the fucking transplant."

"No. I'm not."

"What-the-fuck-ever. You can't make that decision."

"Sure, I can. I'm over eighteen. Nobody can force me to do anything. They can't make me have surgery."

"I can make you."

Tears begin to form in the corners of Adam's eyes. The sight causes me to start tearing up myself. I know what he is feeling. I know it well—that helplessness, the complete lack of control.

"Why are you doing this?" he continues.

"Isn't that what we've been talking about this whole time? It's stupid to continue arguing about this particular point right now. This just means we better get on with the story. We have a deadline now."

"I'm not just going to give in and drop this. I'm not just going to let you let yourself die."

"Fine. We'll come back to it. For now, let's just keep going."

I begin to feel a sense of urgency that wasn't there before. My life, or whatever little is left of it, has a purpose. I have to help Adam find Truth. And time is running out.

Adam shakes his head and lets out another heavy breath. "So far, you've talked about a Knife, girls not liking you, getting bullied, your father being a dick, and your friends not really being friends. None of this really explains how you got to the point of wanting to kill yourself."

"I told you it was going to take a while. We had to start at the beginning, as per your suggestion. And it just so happens that we've come to that part." I take a breath. "The part when I started to consider suicide."

The Macabre Reality of Method

"There were pieces of brain and skull going all the way up the side of the house and even splattered all over the roof."

"Holy shit."

I hadn't really been part of the conversation. But I knew what and who they were talking about. Everybody in town knew. Knowing every little thing that happens was just part of living in a small town. And knowing the big things too. But these gory details were not public knowledge.

I just happened to be there when two of my older brother's friends, Mike and Tony, were over at my house discussing the recent suicide of a senior, a boy their same age, from our high school. I knew the girl he had been dating. She was one of the prettiest freshmen, a girl my age. More than that, though, he had shot himself almost immediately after she had broken up with him. I knew this because Ethan had been there with her when she did it over the phone. So I knew a bit more than most.

But I didn't know anybody that knew these details. It wasn't the sort of knowledge most people talked about or even had access to.

"Yeah, man. Apparently, half his face was gone. A shotgun under the chin at point blank really fucks you up. Closed casket for sure," said Mike.

"How do you know all of this?" asked Tony.

"My cousin works for the county coroner. Whenever somebody dies and they take away the body, he goes in and cleans up whatever mess is left. It's obviously only part time, but they pay him a fuck ton of money for it. I think it's like two hundred an hour or some shit."

"Damn. How do I get that job?"

"You'd want to do that?" Mike seemed disgusted at the thought.

"For two hundred an hour, I'd do just about anything," Tony didn't seem as squeamish.

"Not me. No thanks. I couldn't handle that."

The conversation injected a memory into the forefront of my mind. These same two had shown me a video a few years prior, a video that showed real Death caught on tape. One scene in particular was sticking out. A politician that had been accused of corruption shot himself in the head at a press conference. He used a pistol—not a shotgun like the boy from my school—but it was a disturbing image nonetheless.

After a long and supposedly boring speech professing his innocence, the politician pulled a revolver from a manila envelope and warned people to stay back. When a few didn't listen and attempted to get close enough to disarm him, he put the barrel in his mouth, and a pop was heard a split second later. He dropped to the ground immediately after pulling the trigger. The cameraman zoomed in on him as people screamed and ran out of the room.

Blood gushed from his nose and mouth as he slowly slumped against a wall. What little hair he had was standing straight up around the exit wound at the top of his head as if he'd been zapped with a large dose of static electricity. What stuck with me the most, though, were his eyes. Watching his eyes, I could almost see the life leaving him as they faded more and more into a state of peacefulness.

I know I had thoughts of suicide around the time the Knife showed up. But none of them were all that serious. It was simply a natural progression from the feelings of helplessness and no control. There's always one thing you can control. You start having thoughts like, "So and so doesn't like me, but they'll miss me when I'm gone."

And saying that killing yourself won't evoke emotion in others is horseshit. The fact is, it probably will. People that didn't give two shits about you while you were alive will finally take notice of you and maybe even feel sad that you are gone. It's human nature. So when a suicidal person thinks this, they're probably right, at least to some extent. But the greatest impact will be on the people closest to them, the people they don't want to hurt. The big problem is that it won't matter anymore. Because they'll be dead. But telling them that people won't have an emotional reaction to their Death only hurts your case and reinforces theirs. An illogical or false argument in favor of your point is exponentially more destructive to that point than a logical, well-crafted argument against it.

Case in point—they held an assembly at school for the kid who killed himself. A "memorial," I think they called it. Not only did I see people who I knew didn't even know the guy crying, but I also felt myself getting choked up a bit—although, there was a complete lack of tears on my part. The absolute extent of his influence on my life had been seeing him around in the halls and knowing the girl he was dating. That was it. Yet, there I was, mildly grieving over a stranger. I even felt the Knife twist a bit. To be honest, though, I think I was imagining something like this happening after my own suicide. Thinking about people crying over me was most likely what caused the Knife to twist. And even though it hurt, for some reason, I kept thinking about it.

Killing yourself is a way to take back a little control, to not feel so fucking helpless to enact change in your life. Because no matter what happens, you always have that option, to enact change by ending your own life. You always have control over that.

So you inevitably start to entertain the idea. But it's rare to be very serious about it at first, just like overdosing the first time using drugs is rare.

I would be willing to bet that the larger portion of people that kill themselves don't do it as a last, split-second decision. They think about it before. In all likelihood, they think about it before on more occasions than one can count.

To say a split-second suicide has never happened is asinine, of course. After all, falling into that pit of despair is quite the unique and powerful feeling, emptiness so complete it turns you inside out. Just like the first time someone tries a powerful drug, it's possible and even easy to be overwhelmed by it.

I seriously doubt that his girlfriend dumping him was *the reason*, but that's what a lot of people thought. That's what a lot of people always think. That might have even been what his girlfriend thought.

I mean, come on, right? This guy was student body president. He held offices in something like seven different clubs. He was a good athlete, a good student, and handsome to boot. Why else would someone like that ever end his own life? Hell, it makes sense that girl that broke up with him thought she must be the reason, at least to some extent.

I remember it as being the very next day, but in reality, it could have been several days to a week later. She might have taken a few days off, or she might have figured the best way through was to just keep continuing on through. But I could see it in her eyes when I saw her walking through the hall.

She was still one of the prettiest girls in my grade or in the whole school, for that matter—even while wearing a sweat suit and no makeup. But her eyes were weighed down with a burden I can only guess was guilt. She blamed herself. And I wish that I had known her well enough to tell her that it wasn't her fault. Not even a little bit.

And I wish that she would actually have listened to and believed me.

It sounds cliché and a bit like placating, but it's the Truth. The only thing she could possibly be guilty of was adding some joy to a joyless life. Perhaps she even extended his life a bit. But she didn't do anything to end it. That was all him. I knew I had a unique perspective to give that advice and mean it. But I'm pretty sure that to her, like my other peers at the time, I was just some nerd. Me coming up to her with that message would have sounded like a giant, steaming pile of donkey shit. And it would have further ingrained in her the idea that it was her fault—the whole illogical-argument-causing-more-harm-than-good type of thing.

But I get it. It seems to be human nature to assign blame incorrectly. We take on blame for things that are obviously not our fault, but we always seem to try and pass the buck for things that are. I honestly don't know why that is. It's just something I've observed in my limited time on this planet. Maybe it has something to do with the aforementioned "control" aspect. Assigning blame gives us the illusion of control. A way to not feel so helpless. So worthless. So empty.

The initial thoughts of suicide are born more out of curiosity than out of desire. You ask yourself questions: What would happen if I were to kill myself? Who would care? Would anybody outside of my family care?

Eventually you arrive at the question of how.

How would I do it?

And that's when the innocuous thoughts begin to become not so innocuous. Because when you start to answer that question, the thoughts take a step away from speculation and in the direction of reality. You picture doing it in your head. The idea becomes more real.

I had considered the different options before that kid shot himself. But I hadn't put a whole lot of energy into choosing one. I hadn't really given much thought to the reality of those options and the circumstances of the Death they would inflict. Television and movies at the time didn't portray Death very realistically. The actual damage bullets do to a body were downplayed so much that, even if you'd never seen what a gunshot really did, you could tell it was fake. Any sort of Death was downplayed to the point that, at least subconsciously, you knew the Death wasn't real. Even the real Death video was grainy, amateurish, and impersonal enough to not make a definitive impact on me.

But hearing about how half of that kid's face had been blown completely off and sprayed up the side of his house made me realize that I didn't want to go out that way—especially when I heard his mom found him like that. I didn't like the thought of the mess it would leave behind for someone I cared about to find. I didn't like picturing a bullet going through my brain or blowing off a large chunk of my face.

But more than any of that, I didn't want to end up as a deformed vegetable should I survive, wanting to finish the job but no longer having the ability to do so. It's not common, but surviving gunshot wounds to the head does happen—especially self-inflicted ones because the person usually jerks at the last second when he or she pulls the trigger, leaving open the possibility of shooting a much-less-vital part of the head. I've heard about people that blew their entire faces off, leaving them looking like circus freaks. Or destroying just part of the brain, allowing them to still think clearly but not move or communicate anymore. What a horrible hell that must be.

So what about the other methods? Which would be the best way to go? Hanging? Slitting my wrists? Pills? Jumping off something extremely high? Throwing myself in traffic or an oncoming train? Taping a plastic bag over my head? Drowning myself? Stabbing myself?

These questions led me on an expedition for answers. But this was before the Internet explosion. It existed, but it was all dial up. It could take twenty minutes to download a single page. And if there were any books on the subject, I wasn't able to find them.

So I was left gathering what little information I could by old-fashioned means—things I heard, things I read, television and print media—all of which are well known to embody iffy reliability at best. And finally, experimentation.

My first "attempt" could hardly even be called that. I can't even remember what started me down the path, probably another string of rejections from girls as that was usually what set me off back then. I do remember hearing that hanging was quick and rather painless. I'm not sure where I heard it, but that was the information I was going off of.

There was an exposed pipe in a basement room of our house that I thought would be perfect. Good start. But I had no idea how to tie a noose, and I didn't have any rope except for some scratchy, low-quality rope I found in the garage.

This will chafe and be too itchy, I thought.

This thought explains just how serious I was—or wasn't, to be more accurate—contemplating comfort level as a desirable characteristic in my chosen instrument of Death. But that was a priority at the time, which was probably why, when I came across the silk Looney Tunes necktie, the only tie I owned, it seemed perfect.

Now to tie a noose. My father had an older set of encyclopedias he happened to keep on a bookshelf in the same room as the exposed pipe. I pulled the "N" book from the shelf and began riffling through the pages. When I found the section entitled NOOSE, I was disappointed to see there weren't detailed instructions on how to tie one. But there was enough information for me to wing it and tie a sorry excuse for a noose.

But it was functional. I don't think I lasted a full second of it tightening around my neck as I bent my knees before I realized the "painless" part was complete bullshit.

Had I been able to simply Google it, I could have avoided all that. I could have avoided many following "attempts" that would have ended up more as accidents than suicides, had they ended up successful.

Each time I explored a different option, I knew I wasn't really trying to go through with it. Like the time I took the smallest sip of antifreeze, just to see what it tasted like and whether it could be a viable option. Or the time I put a plastic bag over my head to see what it would feel like to suffocate.

Each time was after a bout with the Knife. Each time, I had the same thought. Even though I wasn't ready to actually kill myself, each time I thought that maybe something would happen that I wouldn't be able to control, and the universe would take over and finish the job for me.

And this thought would cause a weird feeling to come over me—a feeling of peace. The Knife would calm, and the pain would subside. During my exploration, I also realized that pointing a gun at my head and sometimes my chest would cause this feeling to arise as well. So despite my initial disinclination for this method, when the Knife would start twisting, I would point a gun at myself. Sometimes loaded, sometimes not. Sometimes at my head, sometimes at my chest.

After a while, it became something of a habit. Something would happen to cause the Knife to twist. Then I would turn to alcohol and the thought of suicide for comfort. But even through all my experimentation and repetitions, I never fully understood the reality of what each method really did to a person, what each distinct Death would actually look like. Because of this, I remained naïve. I remained bush league, if you will. No matter how bad the pain got back then, I could usually calm it, at least temporarily, with booze and a barrel. Looking back, I wouldn't even call myself suicidal. I was simply developing a routine to cope with the pain. For the most part, I remained sheltered from the reality of it all.

Little did I know a big dose of reality was about to come knocking at the door.

A Duty to Endure in Solitude

"I don't get it. Why didn't you tell someone? Seek help?" Adam's question cuts through a brief awkward silence.

"Help with what? As far as I was concerned, my only problem was that the opposite sex didn't find me the slightest bit attractive. Who could help me not be ugly? Not be a nerd? It's not like I could sign up for lessons in being good looking and cool."

"Help with the suicidal thoughts?"

"Like I said, I didn't really see that as a problem. It was the only thing helping me, as messed up as that sounds. Besides, who would I tell?" I ask and attempt to take another sip from the jug of apple drink.

"Your family? A friend? Somebody, anybody that could help you?" Adam asks as if it seems so simple to him.

I can't help but laugh, setting the jug back down. "Friends? What friends? Family? Like my dad?"

"Maybe not. But what about your mom?"

"No."

"Why not? You've told me your mom has always been a sweetheart. A wonderful mother."

"That's exactly why I couldn't tell her. Why I still haven't told her. She would try to 'fix' it in all the wrong ways—get me pumped full of pills, and that wouldn't do a goddamn thing. Constantly monitor and check up on me to a point well beyond sheer annoyance. But more than all of that, it would devastate her."

I look around the room, wishing there was a window I could look out of. The thought of what my Death would do to my mother still desolates me. I only find the cold, concrete walls to comfort the horrible thought before Adam asks another question, "More than your Death would?"

That thought has crossed my mind exponentially more than a few times. For a while, I drew strength from it. But eventually, it became fuel for the fire. I take a second before I answer, "Don't think I haven't thought about that. The thought of the pain that my Death would cause her has probably prolonged my inevitable conclusion on several occasions. But when it comes down to it, she couldn't have helped me, so why destroy her with something she is powerless to control by telling her about it? I figure I could spare her at least some pain by keeping her in the dark until I finally reached the breaking point, as I did last night."

"Isn't that the very definition of selfish, though? Not thinking of the consequences to others that your actions would cause?"

"Who said I never thought of the consequences to others? I thought about them all the time. In fact, those thoughts became part of the problem."

"What do you mean?" Adam asks.

There I go getting ahead of myself again. That part won't make sense just yet. Best to change the subject back to what will make sense.

"We're getting off track. Remember what I said about precarious manhood? How men are constantly feeling the need to prove their manhood? That's why I didn't tell anybody. Why I couldn't tell anybody. Men don't show weakness. They can't let on that they are hurting. They have a duty to suffer in silence. They can't ask for help. They must grin and bear any pain. If they show any emotion besides anger, they open themselves up to ridicule from their fellow men—and even women, which cuts deeper—and they risk their manhood status."

Adam nods in silent agreement. I know he can relate to that. Just about every male in our society can relate to that. Showing emotion equals weakness. Anger is only allowed because it goes hand in hand with violence and a show of strength.

A question pops into his brain, and he breaks his silence. "I get that. I do. But where do we get this from?

Are we just born like this? Or do we learn it somewhere along the way?"

"That's been an overlying question ever since humans first made an effort to better understand ourselves. Nature versus nurture. Heredity versus environment. Do we learn to behave the way we do, or is it already in us from the beginning?" I sigh and resettle myself. "And that brings us to our next domino. Just how far does the apple fall from the tree?"

The Trajectory of Falling Apples

"I guess he doesn't even really know her."

I doubt I'm alone in this, but certain memories from my childhood stick out more than others. One such memory is that of a Superman action figure that was given to me as a present for my fifth birthday. It was my favorite toy. To this day, I don't remember ever having another toy that I liked more. There is no doubt about it—Superman was my hero.

This fact obviously contributed to my idea of what it is to be a man. Superman is strong, but he doesn't use that strength for his own advantage. He protects those weaker than him (which is pretty much everybody).

I don't remember my brother Evan, on the other hand, ever being too into comics, superheroes, or anything of the sort. Yet, another memory that will be forever ingrained in my mind is that of an after-school story my mother told me about Evan.

"They were making fun of her," she said, "bullying her. Just because she lives in the junkyard."

To be quite honest, I had never thought of my older brother as much of a badass. We had gotten into a fistfight once where I punched him square in the face. I'm not sure how it started or where it came from, but there had been an unwritten rule among us three brothers that the face was off limits. And I also can't remember what he did to piss me off to the point of breaking that unwritten rule, but when I caught him on his chin, he dropped to the ground. Granted, I think he tripped over something while stumbling back. I immediately locked myself in the bathroom, and our father had to hold him back to keep him from breaking down the door. But that didn't factor in for some reason. I didn't realize until years later, when my little brother did almost the exact same thing to me, that I had been lucky to get away from Evan and put a locked door between us. Because I'm sure he was planning on throwing me as bad a beating as I was planning on giving Danny.

"He stood up for her. Against several muscle-bound football players. By himself."

The story had apparently been relayed to my mother from a faculty member at the school. My brother Evan had protected a girl he barely knew from an entire group of bullies that were all probably larger and physically stronger than he was. I can't remember why my mother told me this story, but I do remember feeling an immense sense of pride in my brother.

However, I don't bring up this story to praise the hero qualities of my brother. It brings up a relevant question. Is this inherent desire I have to protect those who can't protect themselves, just like Superman, in our genes?

But wouldn't that mean it came from our father? For the life of me, I can't remember a time when he exhibited this quality. He once angrily pulled me from the baseball team's bench because he thought the coach was unjustifiably not playing me, but I always thought it was kind of a dick move as it embarrassed the crap out of me. But maybe in his mind, he was protecting his son from unfair treatment.

Or maybe my brother and I learned it somewhere along the way. There's a reason the question of nature versus nurture has lingered unanswered for centuries. How can you know? How can you prove it either way? Ever since the beginning of psychology, psychologists have argued over which matters more, nature or nurture. A psychologist named John B. Watson claimed he could raise an infant to become anything he chose, no matter the infant's genetics. He never proved it though.

While we may not have inherited our protective instinct from our father, I might have inherited something else from him.

Nothing really looked all that out of the ordinary as I began walking down our driveway on my way home from school. I was around the age of fifteen, and I hadn't gotten my driver's license yet, so I probably had just gotten off the bus. The driveway was unpaved, dirt, and about a hundred yards long. Our house sat in the middle of two acres.

As I got closer, I could see my father sitting in his Willys jeep—oddly, in the back and facing the rear of the jeep. Slightly more out of the ordinary, our neighbor was standing next to the jeep, talking to my father. Our neighbor, Ned, was very friendly, but usually we visited with him on his property. He rarely came to ours. He was in his sixties, a gunsmith. I used to love going down to the shop next to his house to watch him work and to learn about gunsmithing.

But he was not working on guns that day. His hand was on my father's shoulder, his face carrying a look of concern. My father's face was bright red, as if he'd been in the sun way too long with only his face exposed. His breathing was erratic, and he didn't say anything to me as I entered the range of earshot.

"Your father had an accident, but he's okay," was all that my neighbor said to me.

I sat and looked at my father for a few moments more, trying to think of something I could do to help. When I deduced that I had nothing to contribute, I went inside the house, hoping to find someone to answer the questions that were swirling around my head.

My mother was in the kitchen, gathering belongings. "I need to take your father to the hospital," she said to me.

With not much of an idea as to what was going on, and with a lack of direction as what to do about it, I did what I normally do. I plopped onto the couch and clicked on the television.

Hours passed as I sat hypnotized by the flickering images on the screen. My little brother, Danny, walked in at one point, evidently oblivious to what I had seen earlier as he simply walked into the room and parked himself in a chair without a word.

It wasn't until my older brother, Evan, came home that some light was shed on the events from the afternoon.

"I guess they had a fight. Mom threatened to leave him. And Dad tried to kill himself. He locked himself in the barn with the engine running on the jeep."

Carbon monoxide. Up until that point, I don't think I had ever even considered that as an option.

"We don't know how long he was in there, but it's a good thing the barn is so big, or it might've been too late."

The "barn," as we called it, wasn't really a barn in the strictest sense of the word. It was a separate two-car garage. The ceilings were very high, and it was deep enough that you could easily fit more than just two cars in there. It would take a long time to fill it up with enough exhaust to get the job done.

So the questions beckoned: Did I inherit depression and suicidal tendencies from my father? Or did I learn them somewhere along the way? The answers, however, would have to wait. And when they finally showed up, they would be so ambiguous, applying the definition of "answers" to them might be a bit of a stretch.

The Cruel Bitch of Reality

"Ow, fuck." As if somebody has just stabbed me in the liver with an ice pick, a shooting pain rips through my side, and I writhe in agony.

"You okay?" A worried look instantly dominates Adam's face.

"Yeah, these pains in my side are just getting worse."

"Should I go get someone?" Adam starts to stand.

I shake my head. "Nah, what's Dr. Dipshit going to do? Give me more pills?"

"I'm sure they can do something. And why do you call him Dr. Dipshit? He and everybody else here are just trying to help you."

"Well, they can't."

"What do you mean, they can't?"

"Nobody can help me."

"Why do you say that?"

"The same reason I've stopped you when you start to think I'm telling you these stories to place blame on somebody or something else. I'm the one to blame. And I have been all along."

"Why do you insist on that? That it's not a disease, that antidepressants can't help? Obviously, you are predisposed toward depression from your father."

"Maybe. But who's to say if it's genes or simply the traits I inherited from my father that set me up for depression? My father was a nerd when he was younger. I can't imagine he was much good with the opposite sex, et cetera, et cetera. It isn't definitive proof there is a 'depression gene' or something that is passed down. In fact, the Truth is that we are all predisposed to depression, just by the simple fact that we are human beings—in much the same way we are all predisposed to happiness. Everyone is capable of feeling both emotions."

"Are you saying we can choose to be depressed or happy?"

"To some degree, yeah."

"Then why would anyone ever choose to be depressed? That makes no sense."

"Because most people don't think they have a choice. Because things happen to us, and we react a certain way naturally, and we think that is the only way to react, even though that assumption is incorrect. So we keep reacting in those ways to similar stimuli, and that forms our habits."

Adam's face expresses some comprehension. "Let me see if I understand this. As an example, girl A gets dumped by her boyfriend. Her reaction is that she is distraught, and she eats a bunch of chocolate, which makes her feel a little better. So when it happens again down the road, she reacts the same way, right?"

"Pretty much, yeah. And maybe girl B doesn't like chocolate, and she reacts by watching sad movies and listening to sad love songs. So different people will react differently to similar stimuli, but they often repeat their own behavior when those stimuli pop up again. But they always have the choice to do something differently."

Adam's face expresses some more comprehension. "But if you knew this, why didn't you simply choose differently?"

"Remember that question, because it'll get answered in a little bit, but now we need to talk about another domino. But not just any domino. Other dominos fell down simply from fear sparked at the sight of this one—a domino on steroids.

"It was just one big-ass domino."

One Big-Ass Domino

Dominozilla fell during my sixteenth year on this Earth. The day had been a typical one, a Tuesday in July, I think. Nothing out of the ordinary had happened. The school year had ended, and we were on summer break.

I worked as a busser at a local restaurant, but I had the day off, so I followed my usual day-off ritual. I slept until about noon and then did nothing but watch TV until dinner. I don't remember what we ate; I'm sure it was delicious yet underappreciated. To this day, my mother's cooking is one of my few good memories of home. At the time, and as many people do, however, my siblings and I took it for granted. Unfortunately, it wasn't the only thing we took for granted. It wasn't the only thing I took for granted. We didn't know it then, but this was going to be one of the very last times we would all sit down for family dinner.

My mother went to bed early that night with a migraine, a common occurrence. Bella, my little sister, started to clean the dishes as it was her night. Evan went out drinking with his friends. He was back on break from automotive technical college in Wyoming and was eager to meet back up with his high school buddies. Danny went to use the computer downstairs in what we referred to as the "storage room." It was just an unfinished room where we stored stuff. My father went to use the computer upstairs. Most families at that time didn't even have one computer, let alone two. Then again, most families didn't have a father that owned a computer store. Nonetheless, my brothers and I had been a little upset that the upstairs computer had been placed in our little sister's room. My father's reasoning in the computer's placement was that there was no other good spot upstairs to put it—which was true. So our original complaint did not have follow-up complaints.

I went back to watching TV. There was a World War II movie on. Anything pertaining to war had fascinated me since about age twelve. It was probably yet one more thing contributing to my status as a nerd. I loved learning everything about it—the reasons wars started, the tactics and strategies used, who won, who lost, the Death toll.

I hadn't seen the movie. Judging from the film quality, I could surmise it had been made in the 1970s. I started watching in the middle, but it was easy to catch up with what was going on. The main characters were American and British soldiers trying to blow up a German dam. I couldn't tell you then or now the name of the film, but I recognized a good number of the actors.

They had just about blown it up when my little brother emerged from the adjacent room and walked past me toward the stairs. The fact that I barely noticed him suggests that there was nothing out of the ordinary about him as he walked by. He appeared normal.

Well, normal for him. He had always been a little off. Growing up, he would say the quirkiest things and ask the strangest questions. He was very intelligent in some ways and wildly awkward in others. It was almost as if he were an autistic savant to some degree. We would laugh at his anecdotes, but we never really took him seriously. I never really took him seriously.

"I have to talk to you," he said. I wasn't even looking at him when he said it. I had noticed his return from upstairs out of the corner of my eye, but I had continued watching the movie without regard for his presence. It was almost over. The dam was exploding. I couldn't be bothered right now.

"After this is over," I replied, my eyes still glued to the television set.

"It's important."

"In a minute—shut the fuck up."

My snap at him made him pull back, and he walked off in the direction of the storage room. Almost like stage timing in a play, as soon as he exited, Bella entered the room. I glanced over at her and could tell something was wrong.

There was fear in her eyes.

She moved quickly through the room, speed walking. Not long after she disappeared behind the door of the storage room, my father emerged from the bottom of the stairs and yelled in that booming voice of his, "Bella! Come back here!"

What has she done now? I thought. My little sister was constantly getting in trouble, skipping school, lying, cheating, stealing. She stole from our parents. She stole from our brothers. She stole from me.

I kept my cash tips from my bussing job in my sock drawer. Not very secure, I'll admit, but I couldn't think of anybody that would ever rummage around in my sock drawer. I'm not sure how long she had been doing it, but at first, she was smart about it, only taking a little bit, so as not to be noticed. But eventually, she got greedy and took enough that I couldn't help but spot it. I was pissed. I had worked hard for that money. Even she didn't know just how much she had stolen, but my parents reimbursed me a hundred dollars (an educated guess) and made her do extra chores to work it off. At least, she was supposed to do extra chores. I don't think she ever did them.

My father put his hand on the back of her neck and led her back upstairs. I spent another couple of seconds wondering what she had done to get into trouble this time before returning my attention to the movie. Danny returned from the storage room, and now that I finally looked at him, I could sense that something was off with him.

There was fear in his eyes too.

"Was Bella just here?" he asked.

"Yeah, she's in trouble again, not really sure what for."

"I *have* to talk to you."

"All right then—talk."

"I went up to get some ice cream, and…" He paused, not sure how to say what he was trying to say.

"And what?" My curiosity heightened.

"And I heard something."

"What?"

"Noises."

"What kind of noises?"

"They were…" He paused again.

"Just spit it out."

"Sex noises."

"What?"

"Coming from Bella's room."

"What are you talking about? What are you saying?"

"I went over to see what was going on, and—"

"And what?" My mind was racing.

"And I saw Dad jump quickly out of Bella's bed."

My heart stopped. "What…what are you saying?"

"I don't…I don't really know."

I didn't hesitate any longer. I ran up the stairs and through the kitchen. As I rounded the corner toward Bella's room, I slowed to a halt just before the door and listened.

Silence.

I slowly peered around the corner to see that the door was open. My father was there, playing solitaire on the computer. My little sister was in bed, but she was sitting up, awake. She stared out at me, her eyes still wide with the same fear.

"What are you guys doing?" I asked.

My father didn't even turn around. He just kept playing solitaire. "Nothing," he replied.

I turned around and almost ran into Danny, who was hiding behind me and around the corner, out of view of the inhabitants of Bella's room. I returned to the couch downstairs with Danny in tow.

"That was fucking weird," I said, more to myself than to Danny.

"Yeah."

"Okay, what exactly did you see?"

"Dad jumped out of Bella's bed when I rounded the corner."

"Are you sure?"

"Yeah, he jumped out of her bed and sat down at the computer very quickly."

My mind was racing faster than it ever had. What should we do? Should I go wake up my mother? Should we confront them now? What do we do?

"Fuck this." I shot up off the couch and darted over to my room. I returned carrying a bottle of tequila in one hand and a pack of Marlboro Reds in the other.

"Come on," I told Danny as I walked past him.

Danny obeyed without a word, following me outside and into the barn—the same one that wasn't a barn, the same one that my dad had tried to use to kill himself a few months prior. It worked well as an escape pod.

I ripped off the top of the tequila bottle in a twisting motion that sent the cap to the floor, and I upended it into my mouth, pouring the burning liquid straight down my throat. The burning felt good, and I felt a tinge of excitement as I realized I had begun a journey toward oblivion—away from here. I passed the bottle to Danny and lit up a cigarette.

"They say drinking won't solve your problems, but I can't handle being sober right now."

Danny took a swig of the tequila and handed it back to me. "What are we going to do?" he asked.

"I don't know."

"Should we tell Mom?"

"I don't know."

He continued to fire out questions, and I continued to give him the same answer until finally, the irritation commandeered my verbal facilities.

"I don't fucking know!"

This put a sudden end to his string of questions. We sat there in silence, taking drink after drink of tequila and smoking cigarette after cigarette until they were both gone. Maybe it was the adrenaline pumping through my veins, but for some reason, I didn't remotely approach my destination of blissful oblivion. I needed more.

"Fuck." I stood up and headed for the barn door.

"Where are you going?" Danny looked up to ask, but he didn't move to follow. I doubt he wanted to give up the illusion of safety the confines of the barn had been providing.

I walked back inside to the refrigerator in the storage room, where our father kept his beer. I snatched the twelve-pack of silver cans off the shelf and made my way back to the barn.

Danny motioned toward the beer. "Isn't that Dad's?"

"Yeah."

"Won't he notice it gone?"

"Who the fuck cares?"

Danny grasped the beer I offered him in agreement. I popped the top of mine and didn't stop chugging until the can was all but empty of liquid. I opened another. That one took three separate drink attempts to finish. The third beer took several more drinks, lasting five to ten minutes before I drained it. At that point, a familiar wave of tranquility trickled over me. I slowed down and took an hour or so to finish off the remaining three beers of my share.

We stumbled back into the house to find my older brother, Evan, on the couch where I had been earlier in the night. He was watching TV and looked even drunker than I felt. I plopped down to the couch next to him. Maybe he would know what to do.

"What's up, fuckers?" he said, his words slurred.

"We need to talk to you. Danny saw something tonight."

"What, a ghost? Does he see dead people?" He giggled a drunken giggle.

"No, something very bad."

"A ghost can be bad."

"No, something to do with Dad and Bella."

"You guys are wasted—go to sleep…Oh, good idea, that's where I'm going." He stood up and stumbled over to his room about fifteen feet away, shutting the door behind him.

"What now?" Danny asked.

"I don't know. I guess the best thing to do is wait until Bella is alone tomorrow and ask her what happened. I mean, you said you really didn't actually see anything, right?"

"I guess so."

I heard reluctance in his voice.

I followed the precedent my older brother had set and stumbled over to my room, which was adjacent to his. I fell onto my bed and immediately passed out.

I woke up the next morning in the exact position I had passed out in. As the fuzz of waking up began to clear, the night before started coming back to me. Had that really happened, or had I dreamed it?

I walked upstairs to the kitchen to pour myself some cereal. Danny was already there. It appeared the thought of cereal had also lured him there as he was halfway through a bowl.

"Hey."

"Hey."

"Bella's downstairs. By herself," he said.

"Oh, yeah?"

Didn't dream it. I knew what I had to do. But my slumber had deprived me of the liquid courage that would ease the task exponentially. Reluctantly, I walked downstairs to find my little sister sitting on the couch. I sat down next to her. I hadn't noticed that Danny was right behind me the entire time until he sat next to me. I decided the best way was to just come right out with it. To be quite honest, I didn't even really want an answer— or I wanted the answer to be that it had all been in Danny's imagination. But I was here, so ripping off the proverbial Band-Aid seemed the only way to go.

"Hey, Bella. What was Dad doing in your room last night?"

"Playing on the computer."

"That's it? You're sure?"

"Yeah, why?"

"Danny thought he heard something else going on in there last night."

"No, he was just playing on the computer."

"What were you doing?"

"Sleeping."

"You were awake when I went up there."

"Well, I hadn't fallen asleep yet then."

"You're sure nothing else happened last night? If it did, you need to tell us..."

"I don't know what you guys are talking about."

"You sure?"

"Yeah. I'm trying to watch TV—leave me alone."

"Okay." I let out a sigh as I stood and walked away. My gut was telling me she was lying, but the rest of me was relieved by her response. Because it meant that everything was okay after all.

"Do you think she's lying?" Danny asked me.

"I don't know."

"Should we talk to Mom?"

"I don't think so. I mean, what if Bella isn't lying? This isn't an accusation we can make without knowing. What if we're wrong? And if it is true, she denied it to us, so she'll probably just deny it to Mom too."

The pieces fit; my gut told me that Danny was right. I could tell that Danny knew he hadn't imagined it. But something inside me wasn't ready to accept it fully. I simply didn't want it to be true. I wanted to believe that my sister really didn't know what we were talking about. I decided that the best thing would be to wait and see, keeping an eye out for anything suspicious. I'd try to see anything conclusive for myself while hoping to find nothing. After all, I hadn't personally seen or heard anything. So how did I really know?

Right now, none of that really mattered, though. I turned to Danny.

"I have to go to work."

Implausible Deniability

Adam just sits there. I can tell he doesn't know what to say. I can't imagine anybody would know what to say. I don't know what to say either.

Is it shame that has gotten hold of my tongue? Or guilt? Are they even different?

"That is some fucked-up shit, man."

Leave it to Adam to be the one to break an awkward silence.

"Sure is."

"Why didn't you just go to your mom?"

"Like I said, I didn't actually see it. Which made it very easy to enter a state of denial. I didn't want to believe it. I didn't want it to be the Truth. But I kept a watchful eye after that. I think because some part of me deep down knew it was true. And I wasn't really looking for evidence that it had happened. I was looking for something, anything, to prove that it hadn't."

"That's understandable. So did it actually happen?"

"What do you think? Why would I bother to tell you a story about how my little brother thought our father was molesting our little sister, but it turned out to be nothing? Of course it's true. But we wouldn't know for sure for the better part of a year."

Watching the Pot Boil Over

The next months I spent watching. Observing. Looking for and analyzing anything that might seem out of the ordinary to a normal father-daughter relationship. Some nights I didn't sleep at all. I would listen for noises coming from the direction of Bella's room. One night I heard something. I bounded up the stairs and found her moving stuff around at three in morning. But just her.

After three or four months of nothing, I started to rest easy again. I still kept a watchful eye, but I started to resolve that Danny had been mistaken, that everything really was all right.

That notion was further reinforced when my mother told me Bella was being sent to live with an aunt in another state to get help with her "behavioral problems." I remember a feeling of relief coming over me. If something had been going on, it would be over now. And if nothing was, as I had hoped all along, then I was no longer sentenced to interminable vigilance.

Everything seemed to return to a level of somewhat normalcy—right up until the beginning of the following summer, when my father tried to kill himself.

Again.

Apparently, my mother had finally told him that she wanted a divorce. All his anger and yelling and verbal abuse had finally driven her to a breaking point. His response was to tell her that he was going to drive up into the mountains and over the edge of a cliff. My older brother was home with his friend and took off after him. They chased him up the mountain pass in the family minivan, passed him, and in a move usually only seen in the movies, skidded ninety degrees in front of him to block his path. At least, that was the story I was told when I got home from work.

Then, barely a week later, he tried to do it again, although not in the same way. I came home from work after a day so busy, I hadn't really gotten a chance to eat. I sat down in my spot on the couch, ready to devour my fast-food chicken sandwich, when I heard screaming coming from upstairs. I ran up to find my mother crying and my little brother standing in the corner, looking helpless.

"I don't know what to do," my mother cried. "He's threatening to kill himself."

"Call 911," I replied to her.

As my mother was talking to the emergency operator, I walked over to the door to my parents' bedroom, where my mother had motioned he had escaped into. I put my ear to the door in an attempt to get a sense of what was happening on the other side.

That's when I heard it.

It was a very distinct sound—the metal grinding together as a bullet was loaded into the chamber of a gun. And different guns sounded different—from the specific resonance, I knew exactly which gun he had just locked and loaded.

My father and I had purchased a matching pair of AR-15 rifles just a few months prior. The AR-15 was the civilian version of the M16, the standard rifle for the US military. I had pointed the barrel of mine at myself a few times, but I don't think I had ever loaded it beforehand. It was just part of the soothing routine I had developed.

But this situation was anything but soothing. It was urgent. And until that day, I hadn't known just how well my mind worked under pressure. As soon as I heard that sound, I didn't even really think. I just reacted.

"We need to get out of the house."

My mother and younger brother just stared blankly at me.

"Now! Let's go!"

As I ushered them toward the door, the thought of my father emerging from that room and opening fire on us monopolized my mind. I'd read numerous articles about faceless families slaughtered by a father that finally hit a breaking point and lost his mind. Was this about to happen to us? After all, my mother threatening to leave him had sparked his threat of suicide. It wouldn't be a very big leap at all for him to think that if he killed us before himself, it would be like defying her—like he could take us with him, in a way. Not a big leap at all. Not even a little hop. Were we doomed to become another one of those sad, faceless articles?

I knew that just getting out of the house didn't mean we had quite reached safety. I needed to get us farther away—much farther away. But I had left the keys to my jeep in the house, sitting next to my uneaten chicken sandwich.

"I'll be right back."

I just glanced at my mother and brother before I darted back into the house through the basement door. I didn't give them a chance to object. I took it more slowly as I entered the house. I wasn't sure if my now-armed and presumably crazed father had exited his room and was now wandering the house, looking for something to shoot at. When I became satisfied that the proverbial coast was clear, I grabbed the jeep keys and the sandwich and made a quick exit.

When I reached the outside of the house, I saw my mother halfway down our football-field-length driveway, talking to a uniformed police officer. I didn't want him to confuse me with my father and accidentally shoot me, so I approached in the most normal way and at the most normal walking speed I could undertake. Fortunately, I think my mother saw me and let him know who I was.

"Tell him what type of guns your father has in there," she said when I approached.

"It's an AR-15 with a thirty-round magazine and probably a thousand rounds of ammunition." I could almost hear his heart drop as I said it.

"No, there are a bunch of guns in there." I think my mother was trying to be thorough when she chimed in.

"Yeah, there are, but the one he has is an AR-15."

"How do you know that?" my mother asked. The officer turned to me, mimicking her confusion with the look on his face.

"Because I heard it. Through the door. The slide on an AR-15 makes a very distinct sound when you load a round into the chamber."

"You're sure?" the officer asked.

I nodded.

That's probably the last type of weapon any police officer would want to be up against. He was no doubt thinking about how he and his fellow officers were going to have to disarm a maniacal, suicidal man with a semiautomatic rifle and a massive pile of ammo. I almost felt bad for him. He turned to his radio and identified himself with dispatch, and even though he was probably thinking, "Oh, fuck," the words that came out were these: "We're going to need SWAT."

I hadn't even known this little town had a SWAT team. I found out later that the team consisted of volunteers from the police department and sheriff's office. I'd be willing to bet this was the first and only time any of them had geared up for anything other than a training exercise.

"Take your brother and get him out of here," my mom said.

I obeyed. I knew she needed to stay. Maybe she would be called on to try and talk him down. But I was more than happy to get away from there.

My little brother and I drove around for hours in complete silence. I didn't know if we had nothing to say or just didn't want to say anything. But eventually I broke the silence when I pulled over by a trash can and threw away that chicken sandwich.

"I'm not hungry anymore," I said, as I got back into the jeep.

We drove around some more until I decided that enough time had passed and it was time to go back to the house. I was expecting to hear that my father was dead. I saw a SWAT member at the end of my driveway, taking his gear off.

"What happened?" I asked.

"Are you the sons?"

"Yeah."

"They said you would be coming back soon. He's fine—he's at the hospital with your mother."

In a weird way, I was bordering disappointment. As fucked up as it sounds, a part of me had been hoping he was going to do it—because then I could just tell people my father was dead. Most people don't ask any more questions once it is revealed that your father is dead.

I drove back up to the house, and the police were in the process of confiscating all the guns in our house, including mine. They couldn't take those. I needed those. I didn't say anything, however. I simply waited for them to leave and turned to another friend I knew would make me feel better about the fucked-up shit that had just happened.

Alcohol.

The next morning, a couple of police officers knocked on the door. I figured it had something to do with the event of the day before.

It didn't.

"Let's have a seat," one of them said as he motioned toward the kitchen table. "There've been some accusations from your sister, Bella. I guess the time for her to come home was approaching, and she confessed that she didn't want to come back. Because of your father."

Fuck. It was true. And I had known. I had known for over a year, and I'd never said a fucking word.

"We are investigating these accusations and want to ask you if you've seen anything...out of the ordinary regarding your father and Bella."

I nodded. I couldn't be silent anymore. I told them everything—the night Danny came to me, how I looked out for anything after that. The things I had noticed during that time had seemed small and inconclusive, but they seemed much bigger and more important now that I knew the Truth. I told them they should talk to Danny. He knew more than I did—which now seemed like a pretty lame excuse for me not saying anything sooner. I had known enough.

I'm not sure what I did with the time in between, but at some point in the afternoon, Danny and I ended up in the basement.

"Did you tell them?" I asked.

"Yeah. Did you?"

"Yeah."

That was all the conversation we could have before my father entered the room. I had kind of expected he would be in jail after us telling the cops what we knew, so I was a little surprised to see him.

"Can you believe this bullshit?" my father asked.

I realized then that it wasn't over, that he was denying it—that I could have still taken his side. I could have recanted, just said that what I had told the officers had been misinterpreted. He was my dad, after all.

But I couldn't. I couldn't stay silent anymore. What about Bella? I should have stood up for her a long time ago. I should have seen something and found out the Truth long before Danny even told me, and put a stop to it then. But I didn't. And it was too late for that. All I could do was stand up for her now.

"Yeah. I can."

When I said it, my father shot me a look. At first, I thought it was anger. His fiery temper was about to explode. But I wasn't afraid of him or his temper anymore. I stared at him, ready to jump out of my chair at any second and react—to drop him with a right cross to the chin if I had to. Then I realized what the look really was. It wasn't anger.

It was fear.

The same fear Bella had worn that night a year earlier was emanating from his eyes. He knew he had been caught and had nobody left in his corner. He was alone.

He stood up and walked out without another word. I didn't know it at the moment, but that would be the last time I would ever see him outside of a prison-visitation lobby.

The Blame Game

"So he was convicted?"

"Yep. He pleaded guilty. I never had to testify in court or anything. I'm not even sure what the actual charges were. I never went to court. I mostly just heard things secondhand from my mother. But they gave him a life sentence with the possibility of parole in two years."

"Damn. Life? Really?" The surprise on Adam's face mirrors the surprise I felt when I first heard the sentence.

"Yeah, I didn't know they gave life sentences for anything other than murder. I was surprised. And a small part of me thought it was a bit excessive. What he did was wrong. Very wrong. But I wouldn't have imagined a life sentence for it. Still, it didn't really bother me that much. He deserved to go to prison. He would get a chance to turn himself around in there and maybe even get out on parole one day. At least, that was my reasoning at the time. But only a few months into his prison sentence, he was diagnosed with colon cancer and given six to nine months to live."

"So he's dead?"

"Nope. He beat the odds. He never got rid of the cancer, but he got it to a point where it was manageable."

"Do you think that was some kind of karma?" Adam asks.

"Maybe—who knows?" I had thought about that before. Was it karma? Did his own guilt manifest the cancer? The human brain is a powerful and mysterious thing. It's entirely possible.

"Maybe that was his real punishment. Because aren't prisons nothing but pseudo schools for criminals? I heard the only thing convicts learn in prison is how to be better at crime," Adam says, trying to flip the roles and teach me something.

"Yeah, I've heard that too. But I don't think I had at the time. It's also supposedly damn near impossible for them turn their lives around if and when they are released. Nobody wants to hire a convicted felon. Nobody wants to rent an apartment to one either."

We both nod and look off to the side. I make another futile search for a window. It looks as Adam is doing the same thing before he asks, "He was obviously mentally ill, though. Wouldn't he have been better off in a psychiatric hospital or something?"

"Maybe. I don't know. It wasn't up to me. And I honestly didn't care. I was pissed at him. He destroyed our family for his own selfish and fucked-up reasons."

"But how much of it was his fault if he was mentally ill?"

I perk up. "That's the question, isn't it? How much blame can you put off to things like mental illness or being drunk? At what point do people stop being responsible for their own actions?"

"Being drunk is something you do to yourself. Mental illness isn't."

"It isn't?" I ask, a smirk forming on my face.

"Oh, here we go again. We're back to the 'mental illness isn't a disease' argument again, aren't we?" Adam shakes his head.

"No. I never said mental illness isn't a disease. There are plenty of legitimate mental diseases. Schizophrenia. Alzheimer's. I just don't think depression is one of them."

"Yeah, so you've said. But you also won't tell me what you think it is, so…"

"I told you what getting depressed is. It's an emotion. Like sadness, yet more akin to emptiness. But there is more to it than that."

"Like what? Oh, wait, let me guess—some more dominos still, right?"

"Just a few. But remember, I'm still trying to organize and make sense of all of this in my own mind. I want to make sure it comes across correctly."

Adam shakes his head, his frustrations coming through quite clearly. I continue, "The point is, we humans always seem to be trying to place blame. There are several reasons people do this, but often it's simply to avoid taking responsibility for our own actions. We create scapegoats of disease, addiction, fate, God, the universe, and so on rather than accepting any blame for ourselves."

"So your father is completely to blame?"

"I didn't say that. I'm sure there are a few screws loose and rolling around in his head. I don't think any completely sane person would do what he did. He was even diagnosed as bipolar. But at the same time, he took responsibility for his actions. He pleaded guilty. And it doesn't seem like he did it to get some sort of plea bargain. A life sentence? I can only think of one more excessive punishment than that. Death. And I'm reasonably certain that one is reserved only for murderers. I'm sure he acknowledges that something wasn't right upstairs, but he didn't try to use it as a scapegoat. He didn't play the blame game. He acknowledged that what he did was wrong and accepted the consequences. I can't help but respect that."

"Respect that? What he did was illegal. He should accept responsibility."

"I totally agree. Yet being accountable for one's own actions is an anomaly. Playing the blame game is easier. It's a wonderful defense mechanism. If you aren't to blame, you can spare yourself the pain of the ramifications."

Both our eyes wander for a moment, perhaps in search of that nonexistent window again. Adam calls off the search with a question: "What about bipolar disorder, then? Do you believe that is a mental illness?"

"I'm not sure. Bipolar disorder does have a higher probability of being a chemical imbalance, though, if you think about it. Extreme highs and lows are the very definition of 'imbalance.' I just think there's a problem with calling it a disease. It makes people think that the pills Big Pharma sells them can effectively cure them. I'm sure pills can help, but I've never heard of a single person that has been cured of any mental illness with pills."

"So since depression isn't a mental illness, you are entirely to blame for trying to kill yourself?" Adam asks.

"Absolutely. What I think a lot of people don't realize is there is power in accepting blame. In stepping up and admitting your fault. Because if something else is to blame, you give up control. You can't control what a disease does to you. You can't change fate. But if you are the one responsible, then you are the only one that has control. You can change. You can learn from mistakes.

You can grow. You can't do that if you play the blame game."

I take another sip from the apple drink jug. I'm a quarter of the way through the gallon now, and am starting to feel the pressure of it wanting to come back out again. But Adam asks another good question and I feel obliged to answer.

"What about addicts? I know a lot of people that simply can't stop smoking, or drinking, or doing whatever they are addicted to."

"I didn't say it's easy to control. That's why people play the blame game. That's the easy way out. But it's dangerous to do so. It causes people to be content with the idea that they can't control their actions, so they accept them as part of their Truth. And that is why they simply can't stop. Because they believe they can't. They aren't willing to put in the effort to change."

"I guess that makes sense. But by that line of thinking, why don't you simply stop being depressed?" Adam asks.

"Again, I never said it's easy. There is a difference between easy and simple. Easy is the opposite of difficult. Simple is the opposite of complicated. Just because the solution is simple, it doesn't automatically make it easy."

"So what is this simple solution?"

I must make a familiar facial expression, because before I begin to speak, Adam interrupts me.

"I know—I know. We aren't there yet. Dominos. Let's just keep going."

"Okay. I just need to make another pit stop first," I say.

Just in the nick of time too. I'm not sure how much longer I could have held it.

The Winds of Change

Thankfully, the vodka bottle was plastic. Had it been glass, it might have shattered as I plopped it onto the kitchen table and sat down in the same seat I had sat in when I confessed to the police officers not even a week before. Ironically, it was the same seat my father had sat in for countless family dinners, the seat at the head of the table. Maybe subconsciously, I sat there because I knew I had just become the man of the house—the oldest male member of the family still living with the family.

Yet the tears forming in the corners of my eyes didn't represent that at all. And most seventeen-year-old kids wouldn't think for a second about drinking alcohol in front of their mothers. But my "give a fuck" had departed without a trace. I just didn't care anymore. About anything.

But my mom didn't scold me. She didn't even mention the bottle of vodka in my hand. She just looked at me in a way that said, "It's okay. I understand."

If I had done this a few months beforehand, my mother's reaction would have been quite different. Then again, I wouldn't have even considered taking pulls from a bottle of vodka in front of my mother back then. Time changes things no matter what, but some events can cause a tidal wave of change—turning points that seemingly change just about everything in your life. Our family had recently experienced one of those events, and it had transformed all of us.

Some changes were good, though.

We had a change of venue. After the abuse came out into the open, my mother sat my brother and me down at that same kitchen table and asked us if we wanted to move to Denver. I couldn't speak to how my brother felt, but I didn't even hesitate when I said yes.

Despite the appalling circumstances that led to the move to Denver, I must admit, the idea excited me— a new city, a new school, a new chance to make friends…a chance at a new start.

On the surface, things were worse. We were living in a much smaller and more menial house now. We had perpetual houseguests in the forms of cockroaches and other scurrying insects and rodents. I no longer had my own room, but now had to share a room just slightly larger than a walk-in closet with my little brother. But it was quiet, and we were making it into a home.

And it wasn't long before other things started looking up.

I was so excited my first day at my new school that I nearly jumped out of bed in the morning. Until that day, I don't believe I had ever used the words "excited" and "school" in the same sentence. And like now, I usually had a lot of trouble getting out of bed in the morning. I was always more of a night owl.

Now, however, I could make new friends, maybe even finally have a real girlfriend. Even though my family had just gone through an unspeakable ordeal, it felt like the worst was over and we now had a chance at a fresh beginning.

While I was excited to go to school, I was also a bit nervous. I was uncertain of how welcoming the kids would be. After all, it was high school, and American teenagers had a reputation of being some of the most unforgiving people in the world.

To tell you the Truth, I still can't believe how warm and welcoming everybody was.

"You're new here, right?"

I had barely sat down at my desk in my first class when the person next to me made an attempt at casual conversation. I hesitated for a moment—partly because I hadn't been expecting her to talk to me and partly because I was taken aback by her attractiveness: blond hair, blue eyes, and a shining smile I couldn't imagine a camera not liking.

"Yeah."

"Wow, transferring your senior year? That sounds rough."

"It's okay. I didn't like my old school very much, to be honest. The kids were really cliquey, and they all thought they were gangsters."

"Where did you go, Montbello?" She cracked a smile as she said it, which caused a smile to form on my face, even though I didn't really get the joke at the time. I didn't hear until later that Montbello High School had a reputation for being full of wannabe gangbangers, so much so that it carried the nickname "Mont-ghetto."

"No, some small town in the mountains where people have nothing better to do than act ghetto and do drugs."

"Ha-ha. Well, you're in the suburbs now."

My mother had insisted that we go to a school thirty minutes away from our new house in the suburb of Littleton. She wanted to make sure that we received a good education and not fall into a bad crowd. I think she didn't want us becoming clichés—sons of a convict father, acting out and heading toward prison ourselves. So the school she sent us to was the same school our uncle had attended twenty years prior, one of the top-rated public schools in the state. I think we actually lived in the Columbine school district, but the shooting had happened there just four months prior, so she didn't want us going there either.

"And what glorious suburbs they are," I said, still with a smile on my face.

"I'm Shannon." She held out her hand, and I took it. "If you need anything or have any questions, just ask." Her smile widened.

"Will do—thank you."

I was not two minutes into my new school, and I'd made a friend—and a pretty female friend at that. Things were looking up.

This scenario repeated itself so many times throughout the day that I started to have trouble keeping track of all the names. There was only one exception to the warm welcome. A group of guys invited me to lunch. As we were walking toward the parking lot, one asshole in the group with some jerk-off rich-kid name like Blake or Blaine asked, "Who the fuck are you?"

Nothing came of it, though. I just played it off and said, "I'm the new guy." He didn't really say anything to me after that.

But that was it. Everybody else accepted and welcomed me to the school. Over the coming weeks, my new friends invited me to lunches, football games, and parties. For the first time in my life, I felt as if I belonged somewhere.

My little brother, however, wasn't faring so well. He had been at ground zero for our family tragedy, and it had taken its toll. Danny had always been the closest sibling to our little sister, most likely because they were the closest in age, not to mention that he was the one who'd discovered what had been happening firsthand.

He didn't last very long at the school our mother had prescribed for us. He switched to a school closer to where we lived, which had a bit rougher of a reputation. The friends he made were representative of said reputation. It wasn't long before he was skipping school, letting his grades drop, doing drugs, and heading down that path to the cliché my mother had been trying to avoid.

And I couldn't say that I blamed him. Who could? I mean, what else would you expect to happen after something like that? Honestly, I think our reactions were somewhat mild, considering the circumstances.

A few days before we moved to Denver, Danny and his friend had decided to do a little drinking. At that point, it didn't take much to convince me to knock back a few, so when they asked if I wanted to join, there was no debate in my mind. At one point later in the night, my little brother and his friend decided they wanted to throw a rock through a window. They claimed it was because the owner of the window had somehow wronged them. But I knew Danny just needed to break some shit, a feeling that was reinforced when they ended up breaking a completely different window—one at the high school we would no longer be attending.

The next morning, the police knocked on our door. Again. And I sat down to speak with them. Again. This time, however, my mother sat down with us.

"We know you did some things last night you shouldn't have," the officer said.

"Oh, yeah? And you know this how?"

"We have a witness that placed you at the scene."

"Really? Who?"

"I can't tell you that."

"Then how can I believe you have a witness and aren't trying to trick me?"

"If you did something, you need to just tell this officer the Truth," my mother chimed in.

I love my mom. And she is good at a lot of things. Dealing with the police is not one of them.

"Oh, really?" I'll be honest—I felt a little betrayed. Why didn't she have my back? It wasn't until later that I realized she didn't want her sons ending up in prison like their father, that she didn't want us doing bad things and lying about it, that she wanted us to learn honesty. And when I did finally realize that, I felt bad for being mad at her back then.

I stewed silently for what was probably only a few seconds but felt like hours.

"I'm not telling him shit, so where does that leave us?"

That's when my mother looked at me with a look I still can't really describe. As much as I tried to fight that look, my defenses fell faster than the Iraqi Republican Guard in the first Gulf War. Looking back, I think it had a lot to do with the guilt I was feeling for not telling her about that night Danny came to me for help.

"Fine. I broke some windows. Take me to jail."

"That's not what our witness told us."

Oh, shit. They really did have a witness. Because they knew this:

"You didn't actually throw the rocks—you just sat in the car while your friends broke the windows."

Despite the situation I was in, I had an almost overwhelming urge to correct him and tell him that it was a jeep and not some lame-ass car. But I didn't.

"Just tell him who you were with."

I got it now. My mom had spoken with this officer before they sat me down. Since I didn't actually throw the rocks, I was going to be let off lightly—as long as I named the people that did throw the rocks. What she didn't realize was that she was trying to get me to name her other son.

"Nah. Your witness is mistaken. It was just me."

"Just tell him!"

My anger spiked. How could I communicate to her that she should stop being on the cop's side and come over to mine? I turned away from the officer and toward my mother.

"You don't really want me to say anything more."

"Yes, I do."

"No, you don't. Trust me."

"Just. Tell. Him."

I don't know if it was the guilt or the fact that I was now quite angry with my mother and knew this would hurt her more, but I then did something I never thought I would do.

I snitched.

And immediately regretted it.

"It was Danny! Okay? Jesus fucking Christ."

"Oh my God." My mother dropped her head into her hands as a look of confusion came over the officer's face.

"Who?"

Now I was overridden with guilt. I cut him off and answered his question so my mom didn't have to.

"He's my little brother."

"Oh…"

We ended up serving our punishment by going to a counselor in Denver once a week for a couple months and by paying for the window. I'm not sure if the situation with our father contributed to the light sentence, but I would wager that it did. I wish I could say that was the farthest my little brother would sink.

Now, remember how I said my little brother had always been a little off? His mind just worked differently somehow. He would make comments, and I would be baffled as to how his mind had come up with them. Not scary comments, mind you—just different, almost resembling those of a savant, as I said before. He seemed extremely intelligent in some ways but downright weird in others. But I think my father's crime had left him with severe emotional and mental trauma. It basically threw him off the deep end. Being so close to my little sister and seeing what my father had been doing to her messed him up in a way that I could only describe by telling you another story—about one short jeep ride into the mountains right before we left for Denver.

We had been drinking and planning on driving up into a secluded part of the mountains to smoke some marijuana—an attempted mental escape, if only for a short while.

I lit the joint and passed it to my brother. This process continued until the joint was gone, burned away into the oblivion we hoped to head for. We decided to head back down to continue our futile mission of memory obliteration when my little brother started to act…strangely. He began to fidget, and a frightening look came over his face.

"Are you all right?" I asked.

"I am God."

"What?"

"I am God."

"What the hell are you talking about?"

"Stop the car!"

I hit the brakes and stopped, startled by the ear-piercing outburst.

"What is the matter?" I asked, still not sure whether my brother was just fucking around or had just completely lost his mind. He didn't answer me, not verbally, anyway. He opened the door, ripped off his shirt, and ran into the brush.

"Where are you going?"

"I am God, AHHHHHHH!"

I prepared myself to run after him—but he suddenly reappeared. His eyes were wide and almost animal-like. His chest was rising and falling rapidly with every breath. He looked possessed. I walked over to him, but as I reached him, he punched me in the nose and attempted to reenter the brush. I tackled him to the ground and locked his flailing arms to protect both myself and him.

"Let me go! I am God! God speaks to me!"

"Stop! Just stop! You're not God—you're my brother! What the fuck is wrong with you?"

And just when I hit a point of complete flabbergast, a drop of blood fell from my nose and splashed on the ground next to his pinned-down face. I still have no idea why, but it had a strangely calming effect on him. His flexing muscles relaxed. His breathing began to slow to a more normal pace.

"Are you going to calm down?" I asked.

"Yes...I...I don't know what happened...I feel better now."

I released my grip on his arms and let him back up. We dusted ourselves off and got back in the jeep.

"What the fuck was that?" I asked.

"I don't know."

"Maybe you should lay off the weed for a while."

"Yeah, I guess."

We didn't say another word for the rest of the drive back to our house. For a while, I thought that it might have been the marijuana we smoked, but I've seen him smoke multiple times since then without any reaction close to that. The only way I can resolve it in my mind is that he just blew a fuse. He had been trying to cope with the sight of seeing his father in bed with his little sister, and the pressure just closed in on him.

After the move to Denver, there was one more incident when it came to Danny that made me think, "What the fuck?"

I heard a bit by a comedian once that I think holds bearing when it comes to my little brother. He said something to the effect that if you see a group of black guys with one white guy, the white guy is the one to watch out for. Because you have no idea what kind of crazy shit that white guy did in front of the black guys to make them accept him into their group.

That was my brother.

The school my little brother chose to go to had only a small percentage of white kids in it. They wore gang colors to school. They were the complete opposite of the kids at the suburban high school I went to. Yet somehow, Danny fit in just fine. He listened to hip-hop and dressed like a gang member, and at first glance, you would think he wanted to be black. But knowing what you know about my little brother now, you might realize that he was just leaning on the side of insanity. And his peculiar flavor of insanity drew a different type of person to him. He got along with people that most white-bread suburbanite people would do their best to avoid.

Now I'm not saying there was or is anything wrong with that. In fact, I got along well with his friends too. I'm simply trying to explain him and the type of people he hung out with as best I can so that you might understand how he got himself into the trouble I'm about to describe.

It had been a somewhat uneventful night for me. I was hanging out with my friends from my new school, watching a Colorado Avalanche hockey game and drinking a few beers over at one of their houses. Okay, maybe I'd had more than a few. As was common at that time, the Avs won their game. We hung out a few hours more after the game ended, and then we said our good-byes.

My mother, brother, and I had moved into a nicer apartment halfway through the school year at this point. It was much closer to my school and slightly closer to Danny's school. Like our first Denver house, it only had two bedrooms, so I still had to share a room with Danny.

As soon as I walked in the door of our apartment, the phone rang. This was back in the days when people still had what we now call landlines; back then we just called them phones. Normally, the phone ringing was not out of the ordinary. But it was nearly two o'clock in the morning. This was odd. I rushed over to answer it, to try to keep it from waking my mother and brother. I assumed they were both there and asleep already.

"Hello?"

"Hello, my name is Diane. I'm a nurse down at the Swedish Medical Center. I need to speak to the parent or guardian of Danny—"

"Is Danny okay?" I cut her off. Obviously, something was wrong, and I saw no point in doing the song and dance.

"Is this Danny's father?"

"This is his older brother. What happened?" This was what I said. What I was thinking was, "I'm not about to play this bullshit game—just tell me what's going on with my brother, you fuck."

"Well, sir, Danny was involved in a gang fight this evening. We have him here in the emergency room."

"Is he okay? What happened?"

"He's stable right now, but you need to come down immediately."

I hung up the phone and rushed over to my mother's bedroom. You'd think her door owed me money, the way I banged on it.

"Momma!"

I heard my mother's voice from the other side of the door: "What's going on?" I could hear her get out of bed and walk toward the door. When she opened it, she still looked half asleep.

"Danny is in the emergency room."

"What? What happened?" Instantly, her half-asleep look changed to that of a fully awake, concerned mother, as though she had been awake for hours.

"He was in a gang fight—the doctor said he's stable, but we have to go down there right now."

My mother grabbed her robe and keys, handed me the keys, and said, "You're driving."

I didn't argue, even though the alcohol still running through my veins should have at least given me a little pause. We got into my mom's minivan and drove down to the emergency room. Tears and worry stained my mother's face.

We arrived and rushed into the ER and toward the reception desk. My mother gave the receptionist my little brother's name.

The receptionist motioned to a nurse standing by. "Could you take her back to see her son in room one thirteen?"

The nurse nodded, but as I started to follow, she stopped me. "I can only take her back right now—you'll have to wait here."

"You cold-hearted bitch." I honestly don't remember if I said that or just thought it, but either way, my mother stopped my pending protest before it got off the ground.

"Just wait here. I'll come back and let you know what's going on."

I heeded my mother's request and took a seat in the waiting room adjacent to the receptionist desk. What the fuck was I supposed to do now? How was I supposed to just sit here and wait? But I had no choice. I sat and waited—albeit fidgeting impatiently enough to churn butter.

I wasn't about to disobey my mother, but sitting there was killing me. Was Danny okay? What was going on? Forty-five excruciatingly long minutes later, my mother reappeared, wiping tears from her eyes.

"Is Danny okay?"

It took my mother a second to collect herself.

"What's going on?"

"Your brother got hit in the head with a metal baseball bat." The voice was not my mother's. I didn't even notice the doctor standing behind her until he spoke.

"From what his friends that came in with him have told us, he sustained the injury a few miles away and drove himself and them here."

He was hit in the head with a bat and drove himself to the hospital? Holy shit, my brother was a fucking badass—a crazy badass, but a badass. After all, a metal baseball bat to the noggin could easy kill a person.

"Is he okay?"

"He's lost a lot of blood, but he's stable right now. You can go see him if you want, but just to warn you, he doesn't look too good right now."

"Whatever. Lead the way."

The doctor motioned for me to follow him. We walked back between several hospital curtains until we came to the curtain my little brother was behind. The doctor pulled it back to reveal Danny lying on a hospital bed. He was covered in blood from head to toe. It looked like he was wearing a dark red bib over his yellow shirt. There were about three nurses surrounding him and working on his head, exposing only the bottom part of his blood-covered face to me. He didn't look conscious.

"Is he going to be okay?"

"We have to keep him overnight for observation. Head wounds can be tricky. We want to make sure he didn't suffer any further serious injuries, such as a concussion. We also want to run some tests to check for brain damage."

"Brain damage! You mean, like, he could be a fucking vegetable or something?"

"Please lower your voice." The doctor took me aside. "Your brother was still fairly coherent when he arrived, which is a good sign, but there is always a possibility of brain damage with head injuries. We just won't know for sure until we run the tests."

I felt an anger arise in me that I'm not sure I'd ever felt before. But it was akin to the anger I'd had toward my father when I found out for sure what he had done.

I didn't say another word. I stormed out of the room as my mother called to me to stop. When I got outside, I saw my brother's friend sitting on the bench. His arm was in a cast, but I barely noticed.

"What happened?" I demanded. "Who did this?"

"We were chillin' over at this Crip's house, right? Drinking and just chillin', you know? And your brother started wrestling with the Crip's little brother, you know, just playin' around. The kid got pissed because your brother was a better wrestler and was kickin' his ass, so he yelled to his brother upstairs. Next thing we know, the guy comes down the stairs with a bat and loses it. He asks who was talkin' shit, and the little bro just points at Danny. He just starts swinging and cracks Danny in the head. He got me in the arm. We took off runnin' to the car, and Danny drove us here."

"Where is he? *Give me a fucking address!*"

"Dude, I'm sure he took off when we did. The neighbors were on their porches with phones in hand. The cops are probably already there."

I walked over to our minivan and retrieved a pen and paper.

"Write. The. Fucking. Address. Down."

He did. And I jumped back into the minivan and sped home. I ran in the door and called my older brother. At this point, he lived a mile or so down the road. He was working as a mechanic at a four-wheel-drive shop right by our first Denver house. I figured he'd be sleeping, but to my surprise, he answered.

"Hello?"

"Dude, some asshole hit Danny in the head with a bat."

"I know—Mom called me already. Mike wants to fuck this guy up."

Mike, if you recall, was my older brother's friend and was a guy you wanted on your side in an endeavor like this. Once, during a fight he got into at a party, he took a bottle, broke it over a guy's head, and then stabbed the guy with it. The guy didn't die, but he was pretty fucked up from the encounter. I also heard that another time at a party, some guy was talking shit about me. Mike overheard and walked up to the guy to calmly inform him that if he had a problem with me, then he had a problem with him. The guy came up and apologized to me immediately after. I didn't even know what was going on at the time. Needless to say, Mike was a bad motherfucker.

"Well, let's go then."

"The cops are already there, and that guy is long gone. It's best to wait until tomorrow to go looking for him."

As much as I hated to admit it, my older brother was right. He usually was. I reluctantly agreed and hung up the phone. I stormed into my room. My first urge was to put a hole through the wall, but a leveler head prevailed, and I threw a flurry of punches onto my bed instead.

"Fuuuuuck!" I'm sure the neighbors considered calling the cops from the noise I was making.

After tiring and feeling satisfied that the bed had had enough, I plopped down onto it, still breathing heavily. I reached under my bed and pulled out a vodka bottle. I took three straights gulps from it. The burning feeling in the back of my throat had the familiar soothing effect on me. I continued taking pulls until I felt calm enough to attempt some sleep.

I awoke the next morning beside an empty vodka bottle, to the sound of the phone ringing.

"They arrested that guy." It was my older brother. "I guess he turned himself in. He's in jail."

I felt robbed. I wanted—I *needed*—to beat that piece of shit to within an inch of his life. Who the fuck did he think he was? He wouldn't be so tough when I shoved that bat past his broken jaw and down his fucking throat. But now I wouldn't get the chance.

And I never did. Time went on, and we never really did hear what became of that waste of space. I still honestly hope he was sodomized in prison. More likely, he spent minimal time in jail, copped a plea deal, got a slap on the wrist, and was sent on his merry way. I'm sure eventually he was caught for something else or got his due from some other bigger, tougher gangbanger—one that actually was a badass and knew it, so he didn't feel the need to pummel unarmed kids with bats to prove it. It was a comforting thought. But I still felt robbed.

I still feel robbed.

As for my little brother, he recovered. Kind of. While the tests showed no signs of brain damage, he still seemed a little off after that…even for him.

My mother didn't noticeably change much after my father's secret came out—even though I know it affected her. I think what kept me from noticing was that she was already crying most of the time.

A little disclaimer—I'm not trying to compare anyone's grief and say one person got it worse than the other. Without a doubt, my little sister got the worst of it. But as far as change goes, my mother's life probably changed the most in the shortest period of time. My little brother and I'd had a little heads-up for about a year. My father and little sister obviously knew what was going on. My older brother had already moved out, graduated from technical college, and started his own life. I'm sure it was a shock to him, but I don't think it completely changed his life. My mother, on the other hand, had her entire life shattered in an instant. One minute, everything was pretty much the same old, same old. The next, she found out she had been married to a pedophile for the last twenty-two years of her life. And now she had to raise her kids by herself as he was on his way to prison.

And even though she did an outstanding job, I think she often felt overwhelmed, as I imagine all single mothers feel at times. She was lucky in the fact that her children were old enough to basically take care of themselves. But being thrust into that situation so suddenly still had to come as a massive jolt.

And understanding this didn't make it any less difficult to listen to her cry and have no idea how to help. So when I did find something I could help with, I was more than happy to do it.

I could tell she didn't want to ask me. I think she felt a little ashamed, and I wish I could have made her understand that she shouldn't have felt that way.

"I don't have any money to buy food for dinner to feed us tonight. I don't know what to do."

The tears in her eyes and the look on her face told me this was very hard on her. So I let her off the hook by answering the question that was paining her to ask before she had to ask it.

"Of course, Momma. I'll go get some food—don't worry about it."

"I'll pay you back when I get my next check—"

"Don't even worry about it."

I was honestly overjoyed to do it. It was such a horrible feeling, that helplessness. And I really didn't want her to pay me back. Seeing the tears dry up and a little smile come across her face was more than enough payment for me.

I'm sure it was the same for my older brother, Evan, when he helped her out with a lot more money for necessities than I did. It didn't seem like it was a secret, but it wasn't something my mother or brother felt like announcing either. It was just what we were supposed to do to take care of family. And subtle clues, like a check written from my brother to my mother and left on the kitchen table, were all I needed to know about it.

I picked up on subtle clues to something else too. If you notice, I didn't mention my sister, Bella, when talking about Denver. That is because she didn't come to live with us until after I graduated high school. She went from our aunt's out of state to a state-run group home in Colorado. And she lived there for all my senior year of high school. As far as I could tell, it was because the state wouldn't let her come live with us. I think my mother had to prove that she was worthy of taking care of her—which is probably one of the main reasons my mother bought a three-bedroom condo near the time of my graduation. I figured it was part of the deal that Bella have her own room. I never confirmed any of this. I also don't think any of this was ever explained to Bella. I see a distinct possibility that she felt she was being punished for what had happened to her—or, more to the point, punished for speaking up about it. And I always thought the way that situation was handled was pretty fucked up.

From the outside looking in, one would say that pretty much everything changed for the worse. And if you measure it by most normal standards, that would be an accurate assessment. My parents separated. One went to prison. The other was left taking on the role of primary provider, an obligation that she didn't previously have. My sister was sent to a modern-day orphanage. My older brother had to help take care of his younger siblings just as he was becoming independent. My younger brother had some obvious negative psychological effects.

And then there was me.

Empirically speaking, prior to all of this, I had been depressed. I had been exploring the idea of suicide. One would think that something like this would drive me over the edge I had been flirting with. The traditional theory that one's life being bad in comparison to others' would say that I should've gone off the deep end at this point.

But I didn't.

In fact, the opposite happened. I didn't have a single suicidal thought the entire time in Denver. The Knife was damn near nonexistent.

The depression and suicidal thoughts wouldn't return until a year or so into college.

The Semantics of Good and Bad

"Why do you think the depression went away, then? That doesn't really make sense. Your life kind of went into the shitter."

"You are still thinking in terms of 'a bad life equals depression.' That the former causes the latter. It doesn't. Remember all that talk of control? Well, as messed up as it sounds, I felt more in control at that time than ever before. I had a purpose. I was there to protect my family. I was able to buy food for them when my mother came up a little short on money. I felt like a man. I had hope, something to look forward to. I was going to go to college. I was going to make something of myself. I was going to meet the woman of my dreams, get married, and have kids of my own. And I was going to protect them so much better than my own father had. I was going to truly be a man."

I can almost hear the gears spinning in Adam's head again.

"Okay, I can understand that. But why wouldn't the bad things that happened in your life cause you to feel depressed?"

"Define 'bad.' Define 'good.' What is good? What is bad? It's going to be different according to different Truths."

"But there are some things that can be bad according to everybody's Truth."

"Sure. There are some things that are accepted as universally bad. And I'm not saying that all those things that happened weren't bad. But if you focus completely on the bad, you miss the good—all the good I just described to you."

"Shouldn't I be the one saying this to you? I mean, you don't even sound depressed."

I chuckle. "At the time, I wasn't. I had redefined my Truth. If you look hard enough, you can make anything fit your own narrative. For example, if you only look for evidence of a conspiracy theory, that's all you will find. And that will fit your Truth. Say you want to prove the game of pool is racist against black people. It's easy. The whole point of the game is for a white ball to knock a black ball into a hole. But if you want to look at it the other way around, you will only see that the black ball is the most important ball on the table—and that the white ball has to do all the hard work just to get close to the black ball. Either way, when you look for evidence with a goal in mind, you will only see part of the picture. You will only see it from your original perspective."

"You know," Adam says, "I once heard an argument that the movie *Star Wars* is racist because the most evil being in the universe is black—that being Darth Vader. My first thought was that they were missing the fact that he was also the most powerful being in the universe, and he orders around a bunch of white beings, the Stormtroopers."

"Yeah, I've heard that one too."

"But what does that have to do with you not being depressed?"

I shrug. "Maybe pool is racist. Maybe it isn't. Maybe *Star Wars* is racist. Maybe it isn't. Whether they are or are not racist is not the point. Let's go back to your question. You asked, Why did the bad things not make me depressed? But you missed the good things. We get depressed when we perceive a problem. And while I did see those things as bad, I didn't see them as problems, necessarily. My father was in prison. My sister was safe. My family was moving on. I was moving on. I had moved past the bad things, and therefore, it became easier to focus on the good things."

"So what made you stop focusing on the good things?"

"Well, that goes back to defining what is good and what is bad. I'm sure that some things you look at as bad I felt were more on the good side. For instance, when I had to change schools right before my senior year, some people mentioned they thought of that as a bad thing. Changing schools in my last year. I looked at it as good. I couldn't wait to get out of that little town. And it was exciting to be trying something new. Or when I had to give money to my mother for food because we were poor. Sure, being poor is probably a bad thing, but giving her that money gave me a purpose. It made me feel needed. It made me feel like a man. So to me, it was good."

Adam nods before he responds.

"Do you believe in the concept of good and evil?"

"You mean, as religion defines them? Not really. I think they can exist if they exist in your Truth. We all define our own Truth."

"So you don't believe in religion?"

"Not even a little bit."

"What about all those people that are helped by religion—with all sorts of things, including depression?"

"Good for them."

"Have you ever thought about giving it a try?"

"Sure. But it never made sense to me to pigeonhole it like that. 'Religion is the opiate of the masses,' but I've never had much use for that particular addiction. All religions probably started off as very good things. And to some degree, they still are. But over time, every single one of them has been perverted to serve greedy, power-hungry men. More people have been murdered and made to suffer in the name of religion than any other social construction."

"So you don't believe in God?"

I chuckle. I never understood why people think you have to believe in a particular religion in order to believe in God.

"Religion and a belief in God are not synonymous. It doesn't make sense to me that there would even be existence without the existence of something greater than ourselves. But 'believe' would be too strong a word."

I look over to the spot on the wall where I have now imagined that window I searched for earlier. I imagine the sun shining and birds singing. The air filled with laughter from children climbing trees and playing in the grass. I've been doing a lot of imagining today, so it isn't a stretch by any means. It reminds of the day I came up with a theory about God and the afterlife.

"I put a lot of thought into it at one point. I pictured there being no existence, just nothingness. But how could something come from nothing? So maybe there was a God. And this God is all that there was. There was no universe. No Earth. No people. And if this God was all there was, then 'God' would be synonymous with 'existence.' And it would make sense that it was omnipotent and perfect. If it were omnipotent, then everything would be possible in this existence. But maybe this God didn't want to be alone for eternity. So it created other beings to keep it company. But if they were created in this same limitless existence, then they would have the same power as God did, and then they wouldn't really be separate beings. They would be just like God. So to create individual beings that were different from God, he created the universe. A place with limits. Time. Space. And the time spent in this universe with limits would cause these beings to become individuals, with their own thoughts and characteristics different from God."

Adam looks over in the direction of the same fictional window and I can tell he sees the same whimsical scene I do. How could all of that exist by some random cosmic accident? When he finishes envisioning the spectacle, he asks for a bit of clarification.

"It's an intriguing theory. So when we die, we return to God and keep him company?" "Essentially."

"So you believe in an afterlife?"

"I did, I guess. I'm not so sure I do anymore."

"So you think we just cease to exist? Like before we were born?" Adam asks.

"Again, 'believe' is probably too strong of a word. But that idea seems to make more sense to me now, that we return to nothingness like before we were born.

Maybe that's just because I'm more pessimistic now. I came up with that other theory during my senior year of high school. When I wasn't depressed."

"I think that I like that other theory better."

"I figured you would. For the most part, the theory holds up every time I try to explain life with it."

Adam directs his gaze back toward the fictitious window. It seems the imaginary children spark his next question.

"How would you use it to explain the evil in the world? For example, the suffering and Death of children?"

"Who is to say pain and suffering are inherently bad? We view them as bad because most people consider them to be vile and avoid them as much as they can. But who knows how we'll view pain and Death if and when we reach the afterlife? Pain serves a purpose. It lets us know something is wrong with our bodies. It makes us stronger. Without pain, how would we know what joy is? Also, according to the theory, since life's purpose is for us to grow different from God and into individual beings, children are the most godlike of us all. They have had the least amount of time to change. Kind of a nice thought, I guess."

"I guess," Adam replies.

"Like I said, it's just a theory. And I'm not sure how much stock I put into it anymore, especially when you consider—what possible reason would an omnipotent being have to feel lonely?"

"Maybe you should declare yourself a prophet and publish this theory. Say some angel told it to you in a dream or something. You could be the next Jim Jones or Heaven's Gate guy, whatever his name was."

Adam laughs at his sarcasm-drenched comment, which causes me to follow suit with a chuckle. I pause in thought for a moment before continuing.

"There is one religion that tends to make more sense to me than the others—Buddhism. But that's probably because it isn't really religion in the strictest sense of the word. Buddhists don't worship Buddha, they study his teachings. It's closer to a philosophy. It isn't self-proselytizing. It doesn't say you will go to heaven if you believe in it or hell if you don't."

"So you are a Buddhist?" Adam asks.

"No. I just like a lot of the teachings. They make sense to me. There's one story I heard while rummaging around in Buddhist stuff that I think is relevant to this topic."

I look back towards the imaginary window once more as I begin the anecdote.

"There once lived an old farmer who had worked on his fields for many years. One day, his horse ran away. His neighbors dropped in to sympathize with him. 'What awful misfortune,' they said, to which the farmer only replied, 'We'll see.'

"The next morning, to everyone's surprise, the horse returned, bringing with it three other wild horses. 'What great fortune!' they exclaimed. The old man replied, 'We'll see.'

"A day later, the farmer's son tried to mount one of the wild horses. He was thrown on the ground and broke his leg. Once more, the neighbors came by to express their sympathies for this stroke of bad luck. 'We'll see,' said the farmer.

"The next day, the village had some visitors— military officers who had come to draft young men into the army. They passed over the farmer's son, thanks to his broken leg. The neighbors patted the farmer on his back. How lucky he was his son didn't have to go off to war! 'We'll see,' was all that the farmer said.

"The point is," I conclude, "that it's hard to really know for sure what is good and what is bad."

Adam just nods. He's undoubtedly starting to understand.

Sliding Back into the Abyss

College. I had seen the movies depicting it. I'd seen the parties packed with people, gorgeous women, booze, drug experimentation, and just all-around good times. And I wanted it. I wanted the quintessential college experience. Completely breaking form and, in turn, causing me surprise, the movies pretty much got most of it right when it came to describing what college was really like.

I remember feeling the same excitement the day I woke up to leave for college as I had the first day at my new high school a year prior. It was just like that feeling you get when you're eight years old on Christmas morning. You have an idea of what to expect, and you figure it is going to be good, but you don't really know what you are going to get. My jeep was already packed with everything that I owned. All I had to do was get in it and drive an hour to Boulder. My mother smiled, started to cry, and hugged me on my way out.

"I'm not going very far, Mom."

"I know, but you kids are all just growing up too fast and leaving me," she said, as mothers often say in this situation.

I said good-bye again and set out for the road, carrying that excited feeling with me—a feeling that grew the closer I got to Boulder. I was bursting with euphoria as I pulled into the parking lot of my dorm. I collected my room keys and embarked on the search for my new home. I was going to have two roommates, I knew that. I even knew my roommates' names already as the university had sent me a letter telling me that information, as well as where they were from. One of them was from the Boulder area. Maybe he knew all about this area— where to go, where not to go. The other was from Greenwich, Connecticut. I honestly don't know if I'd ever met someone from the East Coast at that point. How different was he going to be? I wondered if they were there already. I wondered if we were going to get along. I wondered if they were going to like me.

Arriving at the door of what was to be my home for the next year only added to my excitement. It kept building as I put the key in the lock and turned. I swung the door open like it was the big reveal on some stupid gameshow—all anticipation with very little delivery.

Nobody was there.

But the excitement didn't come close to dissipating.

"I'm the first one here. Sweet, I get first choice on the beds," I said to myself.

I set my bag down on the bed closest to the closets and set off exploring. The beauty of the campus was unmatched, even without the perfect seventy-five-degree and clear-skied August weather helping it out. The Flatirons, red-rock formations that stretched out of the mountains toward something seemingly unreachable in the sky, towered over the city to the west. Every building was something of an architectural marvel, each one similar to the next but beautifully different in its own way. Ducks were waddling around the unrealistically green grass and swimming carelessly in the duck pond next to my dorm. Teary-eyed parents and nervously excited students littered the entire campus.

After a few hours of exploring, I decided to return to my room and put away my stuff. After only a few minutes of unpacking, I heard a knock at the door. Maybe it's one of my roommates, I guessed. They probably didn't know where to pick up their keys. Granted, I had figured it out almost immediately upon arrival, but I could see how it could be a bit confusing. I opened the door to find a spiky-haired Asian guy grinning from ear to ear.

"Hi! I'm Doug, your resident advisor." I expected him to extend his hand for a shake, but he simply walked past me into the room. "Want some help unpacking?"

"I think I got it." I was a little unnerved. I may have misinterpreted, but I took his bubbly demeanor as insincerity, as if he were putting on a predetermined show he had been trained to do for everyone on his floor. And this was reinforced by the feeling I got that he was looking around for contraband. Like alcohol.

"All right, I just wanted to introduce myself. My room is over there if you need anything or have any questions. We'll have a floor orientation on Monday, when everybody has arrived. It's going to be great. We're all going to get to know one another."

"Sounds good." I wasn't as good at hiding my insincerity as he was. But he didn't seem to notice.

"All right, I'll let you get back to what you were doing." Maybe he had picked up on my insincerity and realized I'd prefer it if he left.

"Thanks, nice to meet you."

Despite the fake cheerleader persona, he seemed cool. At least, relatively speaking. It would've sucked if I'd gotten stuck with a jerk-off, drill-sergeant wannabe for a resident advisor.

When I finished unpacking, I realized that I didn't really have anything else to do. It was Wednesday. I didn't have class or any orientation meetings until Monday. I resolved to go exploring some more. As I walked out of my room, I noticed that the door adjacent to my room was open. I walked over and peered in to see a guy taking clothes out of his suitcase and laying them on the bed.

"Hey," he said.

"What's up?"

"I'm Nick." He extended his hand as if he had already done it a thousand times that day, or at least knew he was going to and had accepted it.

I introduced myself, and we exchanged some back-and-forth small talk: "Where are you from?" and all of that. Turned out, Nick was from Las Vegas. He was really into weight lifting and his hair. After a few minutes of conversation, he asked, "You want to go get some food?"

"Sure, I could eat."

It didn't take long for things to look like they were going well. I might have just made my first college friend.

Over the next couple of days, this scenario repeated itself, much like it had at the high school in Littleton. In addition to my floor mates, I met my roommates as well, Scott and Dave. Scott, the one from Boulder, had a hot girlfriend with an identical twin sister. His eyes were naturally quite wide open, as if he were in a constant state of surprise. Dave, the one from Greenwich, really liked to smoke pot. He was eighteen, but his beer gut and the gray hairs intermingled with the brown made him look closer to thirty.

By Friday, everybody on the floor had arrived, and a group of about ten of us decided to go out to the Hill. The Hill was a Boulder neighborhood close to campus where a lot of upperclassmen lived, and Scott had informed us that it was the place to find parties. None of us, even Scott, had any idea of the pandemonium we were about to experience.

The first odd thing we noticed was that there were several other groups of students all walking the same direction we were. It was as if, together, we were a herd of freshman. I thought it was quite funny the next year when I learned the perennial phenomenon was actually called the freshman herd.

It only took ten minutes of walking before we could hear it. Just like rainfall or static, a party had a very distinct sound—muffled conversation occasionally interrupted by a very loud yell or group cheer. I'm not sure if I was the first one among us to identify the sound, but Scott was the first to comment on it.

"We're getting close," he said with an enthusiastic grin.

Our group's buzz of anticipation mounted as the muffled conversation grew louder and less muffled, until finally I could make out the exact direction the noise had been coming from. As we approached the party, I could make out several people on a porch holding and drinking from red plastic cups. In fact, there were four houses in a row with people standing on the porches, red cups in hand. I continued to scan and analyze the situation so intently that I almost didn't even realize that my traveling companions had stopped walking a short distance behind me.

"What's wrong?" I asked, turning around.

"We don't know anybody in there," one of the girls answered.

"So?" I replied. "It's a party—don't worry about it." They didn't look convinced. "Just follow my lead, and it'll be fine."

The group followed me silently past the people on the first porch. I greeted them with nods and the popular verbal greeting among our age group: "What's up?"

They responded in a similar fashion. I had attended enough parties at this point to know that most of the partygoers didn't give a shit, and, if the host was cool, then nobody would give a shit about knowing or not knowing you at a party—at least one of this size. And if they did ask, you'd simply tell them your friend Matt invited you. Everybody knows at least a couple dozen Matts. If they continued to press on and asked you Matt's last name, they were obviously douches and probably also hung out with douches, so the party was going to be lame anyway, meaning that it was simply time to move on to the next party.

I turned to one of the guys on the porch and asked, "Hey, bro, where are the cups?"

"Kitchen." He pointed toward the front door.

"Thanks."

If you hadn't noticed, the complete shyness that engulfed me as a thirteen-year-old had subsided and was now only present when I attempted to speak with and flirt with members of the opposite sex. I guess I still just didn't know how to talk to girls.

As we descended into the depths of the house, the people grew thicker until we could barely get past them. The music was so loud that, even shouting at the top of our lungs, trying to communicate with the person next to us was an attempt in futility. After several minutes of maneuvering through the crowd, we came to what appeared to be the kitchen. I scanned the room, found the cups on top of the refrigerator, and proceeded to pass them out to my new friends over the heads of the people crammed next to us like sardines in a can. We filled them with beer from the nearby keg, squeezed our way back through the crowd, and somehow found a corner of the living room to temporarily claim as our own.

We did not get to enjoy that space long before a bizarre silence fell over the party. The music stopped, and the people lowered their voices to whispers. I didn't have to ask. I knew what that meant.

Cops.

"We gotta go, guys—the cops are here," I said, heading toward the back door.

"How do you know?" one girl asked.

Somebody standing next to us heard her question and answered it before I could. "Yeah, the fucking cops are here."

The cops busted up the four house parties by simply telling everybody to leave, causing a blob of drunken people to spill into the street. They confiscated what alcohol they could find and left rather abruptly—so abruptly, in fact, that the blob was still hanging in the street nearby.

"Fuck the cops!" one guy yelled.

"Yeah, fuck you, pigs!" another shouted.

A restlessness came over the crowd and grew, almost like a pot of boiling water, until a fire erupted in the middle of the street. A frenzy ensued. Some people grabbed whatever they could to throw into the bonfire. Others tried to fight them off and protect their belongings, mostly couches. Couches seemed to make up the bulk of the fuel for the fire.

"Holy shit, this is sweet," was Nick's reaction to the madness.

"We should get out of here," seemed to be the consensus among the girls, as well as some of the other guys in our group, which caused us to split into two groups. I elected to stay in the smaller group, which only consisted of Nick and me. The others began walking back toward the dormitory as we stood and watched the chaos. After a few minutes, Scott reappeared.

"We have to get out of here—the cops are down the street in riot gear, getting ready to come in and gas everybody," he said.

I'd never experienced tear gas or rubber bullets, and I really had no desire to change that fact, but something, maybe just natural curiosity, was compelling me to stay and watch. Self-preservation overruled that feeling, however, and we departed hastily.

As we rounded the block, I saw what Scott was talking about. There were about twenty or thirty police officers in full body armor and helmets, wielding body-length plastic shields, lined up across the street. For a moment, I felt as though we might be trapped. How were we going to get around them? Luckily, Scott knew the answer to that and simply walked past them on the sidewalk with Nick and me in tow. They weren't concerned with us.

As we arrived safely behind the wall of police officers, my sense of self-preservation began to melt away, and the curiosity began to take hold. I stopped walking.

"What are you doing?" Nick asked.

"I'm going to stay and watch for a while."

"Dude, you're nuts. They're going to tear gas everybody," Scott replied.

"Yeah, I've been shot with a rubber bullet before, and trust me, it fucking hurts," said Nick.

"I'll just stay behind the cops and watch from over here. If it gets too hairy, I'll get out."

"All right, bro, you stay and get gassed. I've got a bottle of vodka back at the dorm—we're going to go back and drink that," said Nick.

"All right, I'll see you back there."

Scott and Nick turned around and started walking in the direction of our dorm. I could tell they were talking, probably about how crazy I was. I knew I was different from most, if not all, the people I came across. Again, I have no idea if this was the result of genes or all of the experiences I have told you about.

Most people's sense of self-preservation would have kicked in and taken over their curiosity long before mine did. I could see how my roommates couldn't understand why I would behave the way I did. I could see how they would think that I was nuts. Maybe that was what contributed to my becoming an outcast, in a similar way that being a geek did when I was younger.

But I couldn't see myself changing because of it. I enjoyed the excitement too much.

The cops stood in formation for a few minutes before they began their march toward the unruly crowd. I had a perfect vantage point, just behind them but directly down the street from the mob. With the launching of the first gas canister, the mob scattered like ants scurrying from a rock dropped on their anthill. It made a loud booming sound that reminded me of the days my father, brothers, and I used to go shooting back in the mountains surrounding our small town in high school.

That sound was followed by a few more and then a slowly billowing cloud of smoke.

I waited to feel some sort of stinging in my eyes and nose. I was going to take the slightest tingle as my cue to leave. But it never came.

I don't think that's tear gas, I thought. Maybe it's just smoke canisters. Maybe they didn't launch any tear gas. Or maybe I am just far enough away that it isn't affecting me.

They were definitely shooting rubber bullets, however.

One brave idiot grabbed one of the gas canisters, ran toward the wall of police, and threw it at them. I remember wondering what good that was going to do. Even if it was tear gas, the cops were wearing gas masks. Either way, a police officer holding what looked like a shotgun opened fire on that nitwit. His scream of pain filled the air before the canister he had thrown had even hit the ground. Even though his idiocy made me laugh, seeing him wince in pain made me realize how much I did not want to experience what he just had, and I decided it was time to leave.

I arrived back at my dorm to find my floor mates in one of the bigger rooms on the floor. It seemed almost anticlimactic to a night filled with chaos.

"What's up, guys?" I asked.

"Not much. Did you get tear-gassed?" one of my male floor mates asked.

"Naw, I don't think they even used tear gas. I saw one guy get dropped with a rubber bullet, though."

"Holy shit. You're nuts, man."

"Yeah, maybe."

While nobody said anything else about the matter, the air felt different after that.

We continued our party-going experiences throughout that freshman year, but that was the only riot that year. I guess the university had just implemented a stricter alcohol policy, and many of the upperclassmen were pissed about it. That was the newspaper's explanation for the riot anyway.

During these party-going endeavors, a brawl broke out between ten white frat guys and thirty Asians. It was sparked by a racial comment made by one of the Asians. To this day, I've never seen anybody get punched that hard. That little Asian must have skidded across the pavement for six feet. Even though they outnumbered their opponents three to one, I don't think the Asians got in a single good shot. They lost—and lost badly.

At one point, four of the Asians got into their souped-up Honda and attempted to run over both their opponents—and us spectators on the lawn. A couple of the frat guys jumped on the car and cracked every window and dented every fender with their fists. Looking back, I'm still surprised nobody pulled a gun out and started shooting. It all escalated that quickly.

Just like the riot, everybody else wanted to leave before the fight even started. I, on the other hand, was anxious to watch it play out.

I'm still not sure, but maybe my readiness to throw caution to the wind scared my floor mates. Or maybe they just thought I was a geek, much like my peers as I was growing up in that small town in the mountains.

Whatever the reason, they always seemed a little uneasy around me. They didn't outright invite me to hang out with them much after a while. It was like they did not consider me a friend, but rather simply tolerated my presence.

I haven't hung out with a single one of them since the end of my freshman year—not for lack of trying on my part. Not one of them showed any desire to be in my presence when living in close proximity stopped requiring them to do so. Dave even outright told me he didn't want to live with me when I asked if he wanted to try and find an apartment together for sophomore year. It really threw me off, because out of all of them, Dave seemed the least uneasy around me. He almost even seemed cool with me. But I was wrong. By the end of my first year of college, I was an outcast again.

The only good friends I still had were the ones I'd made at the high school in Littleton. But I slowly lost touch with them. Dez from that small town came to visit me once freshman year, along with his friend and girlfriend. He said he wanted to party in Boulder. As soon as we parked by the party, his girlfriend suddenly felt sick and wanted to lie down in my jeep for a minute. I walked ahead to the party to secure a spot in line at the keg, and when I came back to my jeep, they were gone. I didn't realize Dez's ulterior motive until the next morning, when I noticed that the stereo in my jeep had been stolen.

Dez wasn't too bright, though. He hadn't told me where he lived exactly, but he'd told me where he worked, a movie theater in North Denver. It was only a thirty-minute drive from Boulder. I simply walked in, told the girl behind the counter I was his friend, and asked her if she knew him and if he was working. He wasn't, but she told me where he lived—an apartment complex not too far from there.

She didn't know the apartment number, so I just drove around the parking lot until I saw his jeep. Sure enough, my stereo was just sitting in the back of it. The doors were locked, but by a stroke of luck, he showed up right then.

I was ready for a fight. He was accompanied by his two roommates, so I was outnumbered. But I had been lifting weights and boxing. Dez and his roommates had gotten very into drugs and were skinny and frail. I think they realized that, even with the numbers, they were in for some trouble, because all I had to do was ask for the stereo back, and he unlocked the door so I could grab it.

As I drove off, Dez yelled something to the effect of, "I'll see you again, motherfucker!"

It was a weak threat, and I was just happy to get my stereo system back, so I kept driving. It also turned out to be an empty threat as I never saw him again. I heard a few years later that he ended up in prison for a drug-related offense. I heard Jay did too. I never heard anything from Ethan. Maybe now you can see why I don't think I had any real friends in that town.

While I seemed to take a step back in the friendship department during my freshman year of college, I took a big step forward in another area. That Christmas break, I lost my virginity.

It seems stupid to talk about. But it has relevance as a domino in the story. On the surface, it was about as meaningless as you can get. She wasn't my girlfriend, just a girl I knew from work. It wasn't a special occasion, just a house party. And as I am sure happens with many first times, it didn't last very long.

But I was eighteen. Everybody I knew had already lost their virginity, and I was just sick of waiting. I just wanted to get it over with. And in our society, having sex with women is just another way to continually prove your manhood. That's why many men refer to it as scoring. Afterward, it was if a huge weight had been lifted. This is probably why it didn't really bother me that she didn't seem to want to pursue anything further.

By the summer after freshman year, I hit another milestone. I finally got a real girlfriend.

I ran a house-painting business back in Littleton that summer and did quite well for an eighteen-year-old kid. Most of my friends from high school had returned as well, and we hung out all summer long. I was also still riding high on the confidence wave from finally losing my virginity a few months prior.

I met Courtney at a house party, and we hit it off immediately. I was two years her elder, but I didn't care. She was gorgeous. And more than that, she liked me. A lot.

We dated all summer long and into my sophomore year—the longest relationship I have ever had. But it wasn't to last. We broke up after four months of dating.

From what I've said so far, you might guess that she was the one that dumped me, and that that set me into another downward spiral. Believe it or not, that wasn't the case. I justified breaking up because of the fact that I wasn't in love with her. Looking back, I know I took her for granted. I had thought about getting a girlfriend for so long that I had become used to wanting one, to desiring one. When I finally got one, I wasn't sure how to feel anymore. I liked her and enjoyed our time together. And who knows? Maybe if I had given it a little more time, I would have fallen in love with her. But she was essentially my first real girlfriend. And since I didn't love her at the time, I couldn't really envision a future with her. It didn't occur to me that it might take a little longer for that love to come. But then again, maybe it never would have.

Regardless, I wanted to see what else was out there. I wanted to enjoy the rest of my college experience by dating several different women, at least until I found the right one. And I thought that Courtney was just the beginning. It was that age-old pitfall: the grass is always greener on the other side of hill. I hadn't learned my lesson.

Dating several different girls in college was part of my vision of a normal life. It's what a man did in college. How else was I going to find the woman I would one day marry? And as sadistic as it sounds, the fact that I was the one doing the dumping boosted my confidence to previously unseen levels. It was the first time I hadn't been on the losing end. This time, I was the one doing the rejecting.

The confidence boost made it easier for me to talk to girls. As a result, my sophomore year was marked with several victories (for lack of a better term) in that regard. After a while, though, I began to see a problem. My experiences were all nothing more than drunken make-out sessions or one-night stands. None of the girls ever wanted to pursue anything further with me. It was almost as though the only reason any of them wanted to hook up with me was because they had imbibed a little too much alcohol and because I was there—Mr. Right Now. When they sobered up, they inevitably regretted it.

I couldn't figure out why. Why did none of them want anything to do with me, other than a brief encounter? I thought I had gotten over that hump when I lost my virginity and had my first real girlfriend. I was working out regularly at the local boxing gym. I was going almost every day, and before long, I was essentially one solid muscle. I had almost zero body fat, and my muscles were toned. I looked good—at least, I thought so.

And I educated myself on the subject. Google had been a thing for a few years. I read all sorts of online articles on picking up women, talking to women, boosting my confidence with women, getting better in bed, learning what women want, getting a girlfriend, and so on.

And I observed. I had joined a fraternity my sophomore year. I originally didn't want anything to do with frats. I went around to see them, like many freshmen, but the members had all seemed like douchebags. They all talked about getting us drunk and high and laid. And at the time, I didn't have a problem procuring any of that for myself—with the exception of the "laid" part. But I didn't want to just get laid. I wanted a girlfriend. So why did I need them?

I thought that would be the end of it. Then I got a card to attend an informational meeting for "something different." So I went. And it was something different. The guys were actually pretty cool. So I figured, why not? And I joined.

Several of my fraternity brothers had girlfriends; others were very adept at picking up women. I tried to learn what I could from them. I would watch the way they would talk to girls and try to mimic it.

And to some degree, it all worked. What had once been a seemingly never-ending stream of nos finally had a few yeses sprinkled in.

But the yeses were all still short lived and contingent on alcohol-influenced judgement. In turn, I inevitably started to fall back into my old habits.

"Maybe the problem is that I'm just ugly," I would think. I'd think back to that saying that women look for men that are tall, dark, and handsome. I was and am so pale that I'm borderline albino. I wasn't short— about as tall as I am now, barely six feet. But it didn't exactly qualify as tall either. The only person that had ever told me that I was handsome, even to this day, was my mother. And we've already covered the blinders mothers have on for their own children. I even started losing my hair at age eighteen, which was quite unexpected as not a single male in my family had ever gone bald. I read that stress can trigger hair loss, and I could feel the stress mounting as the days went on.

Thinking about all of this made it that much easier to believe that I was ugly—and helped along my natural progression to the idea that I was doomed to be alone. I would never live up to and earn my manhood. I would never belong.

With this, the Knife and suicidal thoughts gradually returned, as did my old friend alcohol. To be fair, the alcohol had never really left. It was college, after all. But the drinking had the purpose of having fun at first. As the rejection piled up and the Knife started twisting again, the fun slowly drained, and it morphed back into a means of soothing pain.

If rejection had been the only thing, I think the thoughts might just have stayed thoughts and not escalated further. But my romantic situation was only part of it. My financial situation had also begun to rapidly deteriorate. I dislocated my shoulder while snowboarding and only had supplemental health insurance through the school, so I put a few thousand dollars in hospital bills on my credit card. If I had known then what I know now, I would have simply not paid them as medical bills hurt your credit less than credit-card issues. But I thought I was doing the responsible thing.

Then my source of income, as mediocre as it was, disappeared. I was delivering sub sandwiches for extra money, but I was involved in a car accident that left my jeep mangled. Luckily nobody was injured, but it meant the end of my job. A man was supposed to be able to provide. I couldn't even provide for myself anymore.

And then something happened that I had previously thought never would. I started to have trouble in school. I didn't know if the stress was making it hard to concentrate, or if the booze had finally killed enough brain cells to plunge me into below-average-intelligence territory, but my grades started to slip. I was getting *B*s instead of my usual *A*s. In one class, Corporate Finance, I even received an *F* on a test.

An *F*. A fucking *F*. I couldn't believe it. How had this happened? I'd never seen the likes of a *C* or a *D*, let alone an *F*. But sure enough, there it was on the paper in thick red ink. Clear as day.

As the debt, rejection, and failure piled up, the suicidal thoughts worsened. They became actions. I started pointing unloaded guns at myself again. The Knife twisting intensified. The alcohol started to have trouble soothing it.

I started to wonder what the world would look like after I was gone. Would anybody really care? I knew my mother would. I could see her crying, and the Knife would twist. I couldn't hurt her like that. The thoughts would then subside, but only temporarily. With every rejection from a female, bill in the mail, or slip in my grades, they would show up again, and the Knife would twist with increasing intensity.

I recommended thinking of all the different ways I could do it: slitting my wrist, taking a bunch of pills, driving off a cliff or into a telephone pole at a high rate of speed. A bullet through my brain. It still presented an aura of uneasiness with me, but it didn't seem as such an unthinkable option anymore.

Maybe a bullet through the heart would work better instead?

Nah, I thought. Google says that isn't as instant and painless as one might think. But then again, that is where the Knife is twisting. Maybe shooting myself there would be the way to go. Almost poetic.

The vibrancy of the days started to dull. It could be the brightest, sunniest day, but it always shrouded in fog to me. Colors once vibrant had faded to a dismal gray. I felt so drained of energy that some days, I had trouble getting out of bed.

Some days, I just wouldn't.

I would just lie there, occasionally taking a pull off the bottle of vodka on my nightstand and drifting in and out of consciousness for hours—staring at the ceiling and shaming myself for not having the courage to end it already.

Yet no matter how bad it got, I never asked for help. I didn't turn to any of my fraternity brothers or family for help. I hid my pain from them.

A man didn't need help.

So I bore my pain in silence. It was like I became two different people. I was a fun-loving guy in public, cracking jokes and laughing. In private, I would hurt myself.

It got to a point where it seemed like I would try to make the Knife twist on purpose. I would think of a time when a girl had rejected me and would tell myself that I was ugly, and the Knife would twist. I'd tell myself I was worthless, and the Knife would twist. I'd tell myself that I would always be alone, and the Knife would twist. I'd think of my mother and other people crying at my funeral, and the Knife would twist. I would keep thinking these thoughts until the Knife hurt too much to keep doing it. And if the Knife hadn't twisted in a while, I would start the process over. It started to feel weird if the Knife wasn't twisting.

The Knife twisting came to feel normal.

Enslaved to Misery

"You would make the Knife twist on purpose?" Adam asks. "Why?"

"That's the question, now, isn't it? Why would anybody purposely cause themselves pain? Why would somebody drive themselves to want to commit suicide? The answer, I think, comes down to our very nature. It's the same reason why I don't see depression or addiction as diseases."

"What do you mean?"

Something has changed in Adam's tone. It's softer, less critical. I think at least some of what I have said has begun to sink in.

"Think of it like this. There is a difference between feeling fear and being afraid, right? If you feel fear one time when you are alone on a street in the dark, does that mean you are afraid of the dark?"

"No, not necessarily."

"Exactly. We feel fear because it makes us more alert when we are in potentially dangerous situations. It has a function. A purpose. Being afraid of the dark, or anything for that matter, means you feel fear every time you encounter that situation or even think about it. It's perpetual. And when it gets to that point, it feels normal to them. It becomes part of their Truth."

"Okay, well, then why do we get depressed? What purpose could that possibly have?"

"Why do we feel pain? Does physical pain have a purpose?"

"Sure it does. It's how our brain tells us something is wrong with our body."

"And we get depressed for very similar reasons. There have been studies that suggest we enter a very analytical frame of mind when we get depressed. We become better at solving problems. People that report feeling depressed during a test tend to score higher than those that don't. It is why depression is often linked to intelligence. Emotional pain is our mind's way of telling us that there is a problem that needs to be solved. And it puts us in the frame of mind to best fix the problem, just like with physical pain. If you break your leg, standing on it would cause more harm, so it hurts to keep you from standing on it. When there's a problem, you get depressed, which causes you to focus only on that problem—which can be quite beneficial toward solving that problem. But that's also where trouble can come in."

"How so?"

"What if you have an ailment that causes you persistent physical pain, like chronic back pain, for instance? There's no off switch. Your body just keeps reminding you that something is wrong. Pills may help a bit with the pain, but they'll never make it go away completely. It's similar with emotional pain. What happens when you have a problem that just won't go away? One you seem to lack the control to solve?"

"You just keep focusing on that problem."

"Exactly. You stay depressed. And after a while, you start to accept it as part of your Truth because of that basic human need to belong, to feel normal. When you can't find the normal you want, you start looking for a new normal. It's one of the reasons people turn to drugs and alcohol. They are looking for a new normal. A new Truth. Drugs are very tempting in that regard. They make you feel good. They open social opportunities with other drinkers and drug users."

"I understand people get addicted because drugs and alcohol are pleasurable, but—"

"That's not why people get addicted." I had to interrupt him.

"What do you mean? Isn't that what you just said?" Adam's question is laced with confusion.

"No. I said people often turn to chemical substances when they are looking for a new normal because drugs make them feel good. They don't get addicted to drugs because drugs make them feel good. That's something else."

"You lost me again."

"Okay, what is your definition of addiction?" I ask.

"It's when you become dependent on something. You feel you need it," Adam responds.

"Need it for what?"

"I don't know. You just need it."

"Do you know anybody who smokes? Somebody that is addicted to nicotine?" I ask.

"Sure, who doesn't?"

"Have you ever asked them why they smoke?"

"Because they are addicted," Adam replies.

"Okay, why did they start smoking?"

"It made them feel good."

"Does it still make them feel good?" I ask.

"No. They usually say it doesn't even give them a buzz anymore. It just makes them feel…normal."

Adam's eyes squint as a bell seems to go off in his head. It's definitely starting to sink in.

"Precisely. The nicotine still gives them the same feeling whether they notice it or not. People don't get addicted to substances or activities like gambling. They get addicted to the feelings the substances and activities produce. The moment that feeling becomes normal to them, that is the moment they become addicted."

"But isn't it the rush that drugs give them? Aren't some drugs more addictive because they give you a more powerful feeling?"

"To some extent, sure. But why is it that nicotine is often considered one of the most addictive substances? The feeling from a cigarette is exponentially less powerful than that of cocaine or heroin. Or meth. I've heard stories of people being able to beat a meth addiction but not being able tackle their tobacco habit. Why would that be the case? If addictiveness is determined by the degree of power the feeling gives you, shouldn't it be the other way around?"

"So why is nicotine more addictive, then?" Adam asks.

"It's precisely because the feeling is so much less substantial that it can be more addictive. It's so easy for it to come to feel normal. You can smoke and still go about your day. And once that feeling becomes normal, which can happen quite quickly, the person has become addicted."

"But being strung out and hopped up all day on powerful drugs can't come to feel normal for anyone, right?" Adam asks.

"Why not? Addiction is not a disease that some people have and some don't. It's part of human nature. And addiction is not inherently bad. Everybody is addicted. They are addicted to whatever feelings are normal to them. And those feelings can be anything. We are born with a certain normal. We want to belong. We are pack animals. That's probably why we get along so well with dogs, why dogs are considered man's best friend. They are pack animals too. We understand each other on a fundamental level. But when we feel like we don't belong, we get depressed because not feeling normal is a perceived problem. So we try to solve it by any means we have in our control. We look for a new normal—drugs, alcohol…suicide. It's why substance abuse and depression often go hand in hand."

Adam nods and looks over at the IV attached to my arm before his next question.

"So people become addicts and get depressed for pretty much the same reason?"

"Pretty much."

"So if neither addiction nor depression is a disease, and addiction is part of human nature, are you saying depression is part of human nature too?"

"Of course it is. Everybody can get addicted to any feeling. And everybody can get depressed."

I can tell the gears are turning full blast in Adam's head now.

"Wait. You're not saying what I think you're saying. Are you? Because that is just ridiculous."

"What do you think I'm saying?"

"I think you are trying to say that depression is an addiction."

I just smile in response. It invokes an expected reaction from Adam.

"But that's just fucking stupid."

"Why? Why is that stupid?"

"Because people don't want to be depressed. You said it yourself—people want to belong. They want to be happy."

"I did. But what did I say people do when they feel they don't have control over that? When the idea of normality they were born with doesn't seem possible to them? They adapt. Adaptability is one of humankind's greatest advantages in the animal kingdom. But it also creates byproducts like depression. Remember, we get addicted to feelings, not something external. And getting depressed is a feeling."

"But drugs make people feel good. That's why they are addictive."

"You're forgetting our discussion about the definition of good and bad. You are also clinging to your original definition of addiction, which I think you realize is wrong. What did I say about the Knife?"

"That it came to feel normal."

"And that is the point I became addicted—when my Truth was redefined."

Adam just shakes his head.

I continue. "Think about it. When we first started talking about this, I mentioned the human mind's ability to rewire itself, to adapt. I mentioned that I accepted that I was a nerd as Truth. Why is it so hard to believe that the brain could rewire itself in such a way that feeling depressed all the time seems normal? Just listen to what I and other depressed people say. That we are in a rut we can't get out of. That we can't stop feeling the way we do. That happiness feels weird. It doesn't feel normal. That feeling depressed has come to feel normal. What does that sound like?"

Adam's head stop shaking. And almost starts to nod. "It sounds like things addicts would say."

I nod.

Adam offers another challenge: "But addiction to drugs is still different. People can become physically dependent on drugs, to the point that if they don't continue to take them, they can get sick and even die."

"You are talking about physical addiction. And drugs can be more dangerous because they can have this effect. It's probably why addiction to drugs is the only addiction people tend to focus on. Essentially, it's similar to a psychological addiction, but instead of rewiring the brain, the body has been rewired."

We both return to the refuge of our imagined window. Neither sure as to where the conversation should lead to next. Then, as if the universe answers that question for us, a couple of uniformed soldiers walk past the door to our room. They ignite a question in Adam's mind.

"But why do veterans of war kill themselves, then? It's like twenty-two a day or something. Why would they want to kill themselves after surviving combat? Shouldn't they be addicted to surviving? That makes no sense at all to me."

"I don't think PTSD is the same as depression. Now, I'm not sure, because I've never experienced combat myself. But from what information I've found on it, it seems that when a person experiences something truly horrific, it rewires the brain in such a way that it essentially breaks it. But the idea they become addicted to a dangerous 'normal' that leads to suicide still makes sense to me in this framework of thinking."

I think back to an article I read a few years ago.

"In the 1960s, during the Vietnam War, the US military found that a vast majority of bullets that American soldiers fired during a battle ended up fifteen to twenty feet high in the trees. There was no chance of hitting the enemy firing at them from the ground. They surmised that the average person is not predisposed to killing another human. They naturally don't want to do it. So in response, the military reworked a lot of its training regimen to focus on actually rewiring the brains of soldiers so they could be more effective killers. Add the horrific experience of combat to a brain rewiring, and you have a recipe for disaster. An extended period of time worrying about whether you are going to live or die could easily cause that feeling to become normal. An addiction, if you will. And when you come home, it could easily be very difficult to rewire your brain back to normal life at home."

I trail off for a moment. I think of my friends that have joined the military. I think of how proud I was of them and how excited they were when they first joined up. And how that enthusiasm gradually left them every time I saw them afterwards, until it was replaced with something darker. Especially when they came home after a combat deployment. After what was probably only a matter of seconds, I bring myself back to the moment and continue.

"But again, I've never experienced that, so I really have no idea. I'm going more off personal experience and what I've observed. My Truth. And how I became depressed and suicidal—that I saw a problem that I couldn't really solve but kept trying to. I wanted to be a man. I wanted to find a girl that liked me enough to do more than just go on a first date or have a drunken make-out session with me. I wanted to be able to protect not only those I care about, but also anybody who couldn't protect themselves. Because still, deep down, no matter how ridiculous I knew it was, I wanted to be a superhero like Superman. But once I became addicted to depression, it became easy to feel normal. I just had to think of things that would depress me."

"Okay, if you knew depression is an addiction, why did you let it keep hold of you? Why didn't you stop?"

"Why don't smokers just quit smoking? Rewiring your brain takes time and effort. And it's hard to change once you have found your new normal. It becomes easier than trying to go back. While there's always a part of you at your core that wants to belong and change back, you kind of become comfortable in your new normal. And usually you need a reason, some evidence that you can go back—that you can belong. Something to give you hope."

A Dim Beacon of Hope

After a while, I started to have trouble hiding. That fun-loving public mask became nearly impossible to wear. I felt so drained of energy, and it started to show in the way I moved. My facial expressions began to reflect my inner torture. People commented that I looked pale, which is saying something, considering how much pigment my skin lacks to begin with.

A friend of one of my fraternity brothers—a friend who happened to be a US Marine—had been telling a story at a party about a guy that put a cigarette out on him. I got the impression he was telling the story to show how tough he was—to boast, I imagined. Halfway through the story, I took the cigarette I had been smoking out of my mouth and put it out on my own arm without so much as a flinch. In the middle of his story. Never averting my eyes from him as I did it. The burning sensation sent a shot of adrenaline through my veins that soothed me.

It felt good.

I don't know where the urge came from. Perhaps I just felt like calling him out on his shit. Maybe I'm just an asshole.

And I have no idea what reaction I was expecting, but the one I got was, "You're fucking crazy, man."

People were starting to notice that there was something off with me. But they either didn't know how to help, or they simply chose not to. A few asked, "Are you all right, man?" But they would be satisfied with my standard answer—that I was just tired.

Saying I was tired was my go-to explanation when somebody started sniffing too closely. And nobody ever challenged the validity of that statement.

Until the night I met her.

By the time the second semester of my junior year came around, the Knife was twisting on a near constant basis. Not only was I not making any effort to stop it, I was compelling the Knife to twist now.

I had fallen into a dangerous routine. I would begin my day with a shot of liquor or a few beers and just continue drinking all day and into the night. My liquor of choice evolved from cheap vodka to Everclear, a grain alcohol that is illegal in most states as it's just shy of rubbing alcohol in terms of proof. It was more expensive, but I didn't care. I just put it on my ever-growing credit-card bill. I would end my nights by doing shots and sometimes even attempting to chug the Everclear while pointing a gun at myself and trying to muster the courage to pull the trigger. This could last for hours before I inevitably drank myself into oblivion and passed out. Maybe this sounds strange, but I felt like a coward when I couldn't summon the gumption to finally kill myself. I felt like less of a man. And in a weird way, the passing out from the alcohol sort of let me off the hook. It saved me from myself.

Not that day, however. That day progressed just a little bit differently. It started the same, with my mass consumption of alcohol. However, as the day turned to night, things took a turn for the worse.

I decided to attend a house party being thrown by some of my fraternity brothers, thinking that maybe some fun could lift my spirits. It had the opposite effect. As the other partygoers drank and laughed, I found a solitary spot on the couch. I watched as they flirted with each other. One group of people caught my eye more than most—several girls with only one guy at the center of their attention. It was Zack, one of the guys that lived there. He wasn't in my fraternity, but he was good friends with the brothers throwing the party. I watched as the girls all but drooled over him, laughing at whatever he said—even if it wasn't remotely funny.

Why don't girls act like that toward me? I thought. What is wrong with me? Oh, that's right. I'm ugly as fuck.

I felt the Knife twist with such a vigor at that thought that I clenched my teeth and winced in pain.

Then I realized something. Nobody had noticed me wince. Nobody was paying me any attention. Now that I thought about it, nobody ever really paid me much attention. Was it possible that nobody really gave a shit about me? Hell. It was not only possible, but it was probable. Of course my mother cared about me, and probably the rest of my family did in some way, but they had to. Not a single person on this Earth cared about me that wasn't already somewhat obligated to do so.

And why would they? I was nothing more than a worthless waste of space. I was obviously ugly. I had dug myself into a financial hole that I may never get out of. It seemed as though everybody else in college was getting some cool internship with some big-name company, thus starting their paths to success. My grades had turned to shit. I was not even that smart anymore. As the saying went, "I had done drank myself retarded." What good was I?

None.

I was fucking worthless.

I looked around at the people drinking, laughing, and flirting again, and it all started to make sense.

I didn't belong here.

I was not like these people at all. I couldn't relate to them, and they couldn't relate to me. I was completely and utterly alone in this world.

And always would be.

Being alone was what I deserved. I would never amount to anything more than a burden on those around me—including the only person that actually cared about me. My mother.

And that did it. Convincing myself that even my mother would be better off if I were gone was the final nail in the coffin. My reasons to continue living had vanished months ago, but now I had lost the last bastion of an argument against taking my own life. It didn't matter how true it was or wasn't. In that moment, it became part of my Truth.

It was time.

No more flirting with half-assed suicide attempts. No more being worthless. No more pain. I was finally going to pull the trigger this time. I'd had enough. I was going to finish this beer. Get up off this couch. Drive home. Take a shot of Everclear. Point the barrel of my gun at my head. And pull the fucking trigger.

And then a strange calm came over me. I felt relieved that it was all going to finally be over. I could still feel the Knife twisting in my chest, but now it felt less foreign to me. It felt more like a part of me now.

Something that I could control. Something that I wanted. Something that I needed.

I didn't even notice the person sit down next to me as I sat there on that couch, deciding my fate. I probably never would have noticed, had I not heard a voice.

"Hey."

I was still in my semicatatonic state, so the voice sounded almost as if I were underwater. Was this person talking to me?

I didn't acknowledge the voice. It wasn't directed at me. It couldn't be. Why would anybody be talking to me? I didn't even bother to turn my head.

"What's going on?"

There it was again. The voice sounded female, and women didn't just come up and talk to me. Maybe my subconscious was playing tricks on me. Maybe I was just hearing this voice in my head. Fuck me—I was hearing voices now? Maybe I really was slipping into the depths of insanity. Was it possible that I'd become so lonely that my mind had begun making up imaginary friends to comfort me? Was I going completely insane?

"Can you hear me?" the voice persisted.

I somehow mustered the energy to slowly look up from my plastic cup filled with beer and see a girl sitting next to me. Looking at me. And talking to me.

"Are you okay?"

Like a form letter being automatically sent upon receipt of an unsolicited e-mail, I spouted off my standard response: "Yeah, I'm just really tired."

I knew this girl. Her name was Nicole. I'd met her at social mixer my fraternity had with her sorority a few weeks ago. I had spoken to her briefly and remembered thinking that she seemed too nice to be with Zack.

Don't get me wrong—I really liked Zack. He was a pretty great guy all around, with one exception.

He was not a one-woman kind of guy.

But who could blame him? He fit that tall, dark, and handsome thing to a *T*. He was also charming, and he dressed very well. It was also obvious that his family had a lot of money, or at least more money than most.

Women threw themselves at him—like the ones surrounding him at that very moment. Yet the buzz was that this girl talking to me now was dating Zack, which begged this question: Why the fuck was she talking to me?

"Come on—what's wrong?"

And why wasn't she satisfied with my "just tired" answer? Everybody else always was.

"I'm really just tired. I didn't get much sleep last night." That wasn't a lie. I didn't get much sleep any night. I drank myself into oblivion, passed out for a few hours, and then tossed and turned a few hundred times until I finally forced myself to get up. I never felt refreshed in the morning—just more and more drained every day.

Yet, despite the honesty in my words, she persisted. "I'm not going to leave you alone until you tell me what is wrong."

What was this chick's deal? Why couldn't she just leave me alone? She didn't care about me; she didn't even know me. Her motherly instinct must have been kicking in or something. She was obviously one of those overly nice people that feel they need to help everybody they can. But she couldn't help me. Nobody could help me now. I was done with this. I'd made my decision. I was going to blow my brains out. I could even visualize what it would feel like, what it would look like. The thought of a bullet barreling through my head with such force that it splattered blood, skull, and brain matter all over my wall as my body went limp didn't seem like such a bad thing anymore. It even soothed me now, the picture of my lifeless eyes half-open and staring into space, looking as if they had finally found peace.

Still, I'll admit it was a little nice that somebody had finally noticed me.

"Look, I'm fine. It's a party. Everybody is having fun. You should too. Nothing is wrong."

"Like I said, I'm just going to sit here until you talk to me."

She wasn't going to give up. I would be dead in no more than a couple hours, so what would it hurt to give her a little story, so she'd leave me alone? I didn't have to tell her everything. I didn't have to tell her much at all. Screw it. I didn't even know this girl. I was going to turn the questions back on her.

"Aren't you dating Zack?" I motioned to Zack, still surrounded by his harem of groupies.

"No. Zack and I aren't dating."

"That's not what people are saying."

"Well, people say a lot of things that aren't true."

"Yeah, but rumors have to start somewhere. There's usually at least some Truth to them."

"Yes. I went out with Zack a couple of times, but look at him over there. What kind of boyfriend would that be? I would always be wondering where he was, what he was doing—or more accurately, *who* he was doing."

I was taken aback when I cracked a half smile. How did she just make me smile? I hadn't smiled in so long that it felt strange. Foreign. Unpleasant.

"I guess you're right about that."

"So what's up with you? Why are you sitting on this couch by yourself, looking all sad? Why aren't you out there chatting up the girls?"

Why was I not out there chatting up the girls? The same reason I didn't go around pissing on electric fences. Neither would have a positive result.

I grimaced. "Why are you sitting here talking to the guy on the couch and not out there chatting up the guys?"

"Touché, good sir. You just looked like you could use a friend to talk to."

"What made you think that?"

"We all need a friend sometimes, myself included. So I guess I just recognized the look."

She recognized the look? You know, despite trying to hide my pain for so long, I still secretly hoped somebody would notice. I didn't know how that would work since I still didn't want anybody to know—I still didn't want the inevitable pity.

But that had been before I realized that no one could help—before I realized that I was always going to be alone.

"So what's wrong?" she pressed.

"You really aren't going to leave me alone, are you?"

"Nope."

Well, I better tell her something then. Get rid of her. "I'm just having some family trouble."

"What kind of family trouble?"

"My father's a dick."

Oh shit. I didn't mean to say that. I meant to tell her he had cancer or that we'd had some financial troubles, or even to simply invent some other tragedy that normally befalls a family, like somebody dying. That would have been so much more harmless because it would've limited the number of follow-up questions. What kind of cancer? How long did the doctor give him? Most people would even just say, "I'm sorry to hear that," so I could reply with, "It's okay—I'm dealing with it," and the discussion would be over. But my statement opened doors to all sorts of questions: Is he an alcoholic? Does he do drugs? Does he beat you? Does he beat your mother? Does he molest you?

Does he molest your siblings?

This was a question I didn't want to answer, an avenue I didn't want to explore. Yet I was the one that opened the door. Why did I do that? Why did I unlock the gate, allowing this flood of a discussion I didn't want to have to rush over me, drowning me as I wished for a take back? Or even worse, she could express pity for me. For fuck's sake, I hoped that didn't happen.

For some reason, however, her response was not invasive. It did not express pity. She simply said, "My father can be a dick too."

Crisis averted. She had taken another route I hadn't foreseen. She'd empathized with me. Empathy was not the same thing as sympathy. When you're sympathizing, you are looking down. When you're empathizing, you are looking straight across. I was okay with somebody looking straight across at me; it was the looking-down thing that got me when it came to sympathy. To pity.

We both paused for a second, neither really knowing what to say next. I figured that I'd officially scared this girl off and that at any moment she would get up and leave. For a brief moment, I felt satisfied from accomplishing my goal. Almost instantly, however, that satisfaction turned to pain from the Knife twisting in my chest; her walking off would further support my idea that nobody did or ever would care about me…I winced again.

"What's wrong?"

"Heartburn, I guess."   I was quick with the answer, and because of that, I think she accepted it—or at least didn't challenge it.

But she was still sitting there.

"Okay, I told you what was wrong. Why are you still sitting here?"

"Because you started your story. You didn't end it."

"Jesus, what are you, a shrink? You just sit there, saying almost nothing in the hopes that I'll let all of my skeletons out of the closet and expose them to a complete stranger?"

"If you want to look at it that way, fine. I think it's just two friends talking about what's bothering them."

"Friends? I don't even know you."

"We have many mutual friends. That makes us friends by association…kind of like in-laws."

"You really are something else, aren't you?"

"Yup." She smiled.

We paused again, but this time when our eyes met, they locked. I suspected my eyes were filled with confusion and pain. Her eyes emanated nothing but a beautiful compassion, captivating me with it. Even though we'd been talking for several minutes now, and I had met her a few weeks before, this was the first time I'd realized how beautiful she was. She was so gorgeous that I can't describe it to you without getting poetically mushy. Golden locks of angelic hair. Eyes that would make a sunset weep with envy. A smile so infectious that it made me smile for the second time in months. And this time, it was a full smile. It still felt weird, though. I wiped it from my face and quickly looked away again.

"How did you just do that?" I asked.

"Do what?"

"Make me smile."

"I was all state in making people smile in high school. That and underwater basket weaving."

I smiled again. "Stop it."

She made a funny face, and my smile opened into a chuckle.

"Seriously, knock it off."

She made another funny face, and my chuckle turned into a mild laugh. Damn, this felt awkward. Veritably unpleasant. It had become so foreign. Laughing even caused physical pain in my head.

The laughing dissipated, and my brief headache subsided within a matter of seconds. Yet, there was one other side effect from the laughing.

The Knife stopped twisting.

I could still feel it there. I still had that knot in my chest. But it was much more bearable now as it wasn't rotating.

"Feel better?" she asked.

"Actually, I do. Thank you."

"Anytime, Sunshine. So you ready to come back to the party?"

"No, I'm still good right here."

"All right, well, I guess I'll stay here with you, then. I can mope too, you know?"

Her mouth formed a false frown, and I chuckled again.

"You are a very strange person, you know that?"

"Says the guy on the couch. Are you going to tell me what's really bothering you now, or am I going to have to beat it out of ya?" Her hands formed fists that she waved menacingly at me.

I smiled again and said, "You really don't want to hear it—trust me."

"No, I really do."

Maybe it was something in her voice. Maybe it was her beauty. Maybe it was her wit and the fact that she had made me laugh, a seemingly insurmountable task. Maybe subconsciously, I simply felt I needed to open up to somebody, to let it out. I'm not sure what it was at that moment that allowed me to open up to her. All I know is that I told her things I had never told anybody before.

I told her about my father and the horrible thing he had done. I told her how I still carried guilt for not protecting my little sister. I told her about my woes with women and finances. I told her how I would drink to kill the pain and how, most days, I had trouble mustering the energy just to get out of bed. I told her almost everything. The only part I left out was the part about my suicidal thoughts and attempts and how, up until a few minutes ago, I had decided that I was going to finish the job—that night. I guess I was afraid that she might try and stop me. I didn't look at her as I spoke. I couldn't bring myself to look into those eyes while telling that story. I just stared straight ahead and talked.

When I finished with my story, I looked over at her, half expecting to see an empty seat where she had been sitting. Yet, she was still there, just looking at me with an expression on her face to suggest that she had listened to every word I'd just said. And she was still listening. Hesitating to make sure I was finished, she leaned over and hugged me. I almost started to cry when she did so. I couldn't remember the last time anybody other than my mother had hugged me. I don't even think the women I had slept with had just hugged me at any point.

The cold steel of the Knife warmed at her touch. I felt at peace in her arms, safety, as if this monster that had engulfed my existence were suddenly held at bay. When she released her gentle grip, I instantly yearned for its return.

"I would appreciate it if you kept what I just told you between you and me."

She smiled as she ran her fingers across her lips, metaphorically zipping them shut. "Of course."

"I feel like kissing you right now." I'm not sure where that came from. I think I meant to just think it, not to say it out loud. I was instantly stricken with embarrassment and wished for another take back.

But she didn't say no. She didn't make a face of disgust or disdain. She looked over at Zack a few yards away and then back to me.

"I don't think this is really a good place for that."

"I know. I just feel like doing it—I didn't say I was going to. I really am tired, though. I should be on my way home."

"Okay."

"Thank you."

"Call me tomorrow," she said. "We'll go do something fun."

We exchanged phone numbers before she hugged me again. We parted ways, and I drove back to my house. When I got to my room, I looked over at the rifle in the closet, sitting just underneath the bottle of Everclear on the shelf.

"I don't need you tonight. Either of you." I don't remember if I said it aloud or just thought it.

I lay down on my bed, closed my eyes, and for the first time in months, simply fell asleep.

In the morning, I felt refreshed, renewed. I didn't have to work up the energy to get out of bed. I had a headache, and I felt hungover. But I didn't have the urge to take my morning pull from the bottle of Everclear.

What did that girl do to me last night? I hesitated for a moment.

She saved my life.

The thought popped into my head as if somebody else had planted it there.

But there was no doubt in my mind. If she hadn't sat down next to me, if she hadn't made me laugh, listened to me, hugged me, shown interest in me…I would be dead. I would have shot myself in the head with the rifle in the closet. I was still alive because of her. A feeling of warmth came over me at the thought of talking to her again, seeing her again. I had the urge to pick up the phone and call her right then.

But I didn't.

Because the feeling of gratitude quickly morphed into a feeling of fear. Fear that I was going to do something to push her away from me. Fear that I would inevitably fuck it up somehow, as I always did. Fear that maybe her empathy really was sympathy and that she actually looked down on me. Fear that she didn't respect me.

How could she respect me? I poured my heart out to her. I showed weakness. I couldn't call her.

I grabbed my towel, walked to the bathroom, and took a shower. I walked back to my room and started to dress myself, the urge to take a pull from the Everclear bottle growing.

Then my cell phone rang. The name on the phone?

Nicole.

Holy shit, she was calling me. I let the surprise subside for two more rings before I answered. "Hello?"

"Hey."

"Hey, how's it going?"

"I'm good. Are you feeling better today?"

"Yes, I am, actually. Thanks for asking."

"Better enough to come to the Celestial Seasonings factory with me today?"

"What would we do there?"

"Drink tea, have fun."

"I don't have much money…"

"Well, that would be a problem if it weren't free."

"Really?"

"See? Now you have no more excuses left. Pick you up at your house in an hour?"

"Sure, I guess."

"Great! See you then."

I hung up the phone, still a bit bewildered at what had just happened. "Did she just ask me out?" I asked myself. "I think she did." In my entire life, I had never been asked out by a girl. What kind of twilight zone had I entered? Did I actually kill myself the other night, and this was the afterlife?

I was jumping to conclusions. This wasn't an actual date. It couldn't be. She just wanted to go to the tea factory, and I was probably the only person to say yes. She'd probably asked no fewer than ten people before she called me.

Still. She called me. She thought of me, something that I couldn't remember ever happening before. The euphoria derived from this thought was fleeting, however. It promptly transformed back into fear.

What if this really was a date? I really liked this girl. I didn't want to fuck it up. But if history was any indicator, I was going to. It was inescapable. I should just call her back and cancel. I couldn't do this. I couldn't fuck up the one good thing that had happened to me in as long as I could remember.

Then again, canceling might've been just be the way I was going to fuck it up. I was fucked if I did, fucked if I didn't.

I gave myself a good smack on the right cheek. "Get the fuck ahold of yourself. You got this."

Deep breath.

Okay. I had this. I'd been on dates before. This was no different.

Except that it was.

This girl was amazing. I'd never met anyone like her. I couldn't even express how much I didn't want to screw it up, and I'd screwed up every other romantic encounter until then. How could I have even the slightest hint of hope that I wasn't going to screw this up too somehow?

I had to try.

I took a couple deep breaths. The calming effect invited the excitement back in. Even if she didn't consider this a date, I got to hang out with the coolest girl I'd ever met. And she had initiated all of it.

Looking back, I'm thankful for the fear. It tempered my excitement and helped keep me from making a complete fool of myself.

The smile on her face as she walked down the hall toward my room induced a feeling of warmth I couldn't quite describe—like a soft blanket or a hug from your mother after you've scraped your knee. Looking at that smile, I felt at peace. I felt safe.

"Ready?"

"As ready as I'll ever be."

I wouldn't have thought a tea factory would have been so fun to visit, but it was. I had never realized how much peppermint can sting your eyes until I went into the peppermint room. We both cracked jokes and made each other laugh. It was so natural, being with her. Maybe the fun of the tea factory was due in large part to the company.

Okay, not maybe.

Definitely.

This girl couldn't be real. I was already dead. I had summoned the strength to shoot myself, and somehow, someway, I had been granted entrance to heaven.

There was no other logical explanation for a girl this amazing choosing to spend time with me. Regardless of my logical mind attempting to make sense of it, I had a perpetual smile on my face.

And everything was so natural. Every little bit of fear was washed away before I could feel it. It was one of the best days I'd ever had in my life—just going to a tea factory.

We got back to my room, and I figured I'd still find a way to fuck it up. It was inevitable. I had to fuck this up somehow.

And then my phone rang.

It was my mother. And I could never help but answer the phone when my mom called. She started talking about something that didn't matter in the slightest, and I was trying to pay attention. And then Nicole said something to the effect that she was going to leave and let me talk to my mom.

Something inside me took over. I threw the phone on the bed. I grabbed Nicole around the waist with one arm and cradled the side of her face with my other hand. And I kissed her. She slowly pulled away after, looking at me with that amazing smile of hers.

"Call me," was all she said.

"Isn't that a bit of a given?"

She smiled and turned to leave. I watched her walk away, and right before she got to the stairs, she skipped and clicked her heels. This couldn't be real life. This shit only happened in the movies.

I picked up the phone to find my mother hadn't even noticed and was still just talking away. I waited for her to finish her tirade. When finally she asked me, "What's new with you?" I didn't even think—I just blurted out, "I just met the most amazing girl."

I immediately regretted it. I'd been on one date with this girl. I shouldn't be telling my mom about her yet. But I doubted even a fire hose could have washed the smile off my face.

"Really?"

I could almost feel the joy emanating from mother. "It's still early, but she really is amazing, Mom."

"I'm so happy for you. I always knew you would find the girl for you. I worried about your brothers and sister, but I knew you would find her."

"That's extremely premature, Mom, but I'll keep you updated."

The next few weeks were some of the happiest weeks I'd had in longer than I could remember. Nicole and I hung out pretty much every day. We cracked jokes. We laughed. She recommended books and other things she figured could help me with my depression. She really seemed to genuinely care about me.

Sometimes I think I'm the dumbest smart person I know.

Journey to the Bottom Rock

I wish I could say that hindsight is twenty-twenty, but even at the time, I knew that this infatuation was dangerous. I knew it wasn't reciprocated, not really. But denial is a powerful thing, especially when one is already falling and grasping for anything to hold on to.

I allowed myself to speculate, to picture this working out as something other than what always happened. And the only thing that accomplished was lifting myself a little higher so I could fall farther.

I must have watched too many romantic comedies to think that it was going to end any other way than the way it did.

It didn't take long. A party a few weeks later was the beginning of the end. I was foolish to think that she would've been excited to see me upon arrival. But she didn't even make her presence known to me. I didn't even realize she was there until I walked into the hall and saw her kissing one of my fraternity brothers.

Wow. That word is overused I think. People say it all the time and usually don't come close to utilizing the true meaning of the word.

But I think I did when I said it then.

Neither one noticed me. I didn't make my presence known. I don't think it would have mattered if I had.

The next day, she played it off like it had never happened. She called me and inquired about hanging out again. And just about everything in me wanted to go along with that—to forget what I had seen.

But I couldn't.

I couldn't unsee it. But I also couldn't bring myself to confront her about it. I couldn't risk her cutting me out of her life, even though a significant part of me wanted to cut her out of mine.

What the fuck should I have done?

I don't believe I've ever been that unsure about anything. I didn't want to push her away, but at the same time, I didn't want to be second choice. I was infatuated with her, but if that wasn't the same for her, I knew it was time to bail.

"I really like you."

This is what she said to me. And I believed it. I wanted to believe it. But it wasn't true.

I've always been cursed with this brain, a brain that works better than others'—as much as I've tried to kill it or make it more normal by drowning it in alcohol. It hasn't worked. And I wish there were another explanation.

But the next time I saw the girl, she was hanging out with one of my other fraternity brothers, one of those guys that women threw themselves at. The guy was basically a Ken doll. He told me later that she dropped her pants and basically begged him to fuck her.

He said he didn't. I still don't know how much of the story I believe, but it doesn't really matter. I couldn't possibly blame him if he did. She wasn't my girlfriend. But I, at the very least, believe that she did what he said she did. And that should have been enough for me to just consider her a bitch and move on.

But the timing.

This girl had saved my life. And now she was just like every other girl I'd ever come across. Why? Why did she even bother saving my life? Why didn't she just let me do it? The only explanation that made sense to me was that this was the universe just fucking with me again. It knew I would swoon at this girl, and it wanted to see just how badly it could fuck me up. Just how pissed off could a human being get?

I tried to calm myself. I tried to tell myself that this had been inevitable, and I had known that. But it didn't calm that fire raging inside me. So, in my futile attempt to do so, I went to the yard. I began punching off the tops of the fence posts, and slowly, it started to make me feel better. I knew that feeling was going to be short lived, but the only other alternative was to shoot myself in the head. And that idea kept popping into my mind, but this girl had fucked with my way of thinking. She had introduced a desire to live into the mix, something that I had done away with a while ago.

This had to be the universe just fucking with me. It knew I was on the brink, so it introduced me to this bitch and made me think for a moment that I was wrong, that I wasn't doomed to be alone and in pain for the rest of my short, pathetic excuse for a life. And now it was laughing its fucking ass off.

Well played, universe. Well played. You fuck.

You held me off for a spell. But this shit is inevitable, isn't it?

I just sank deeper and deeper into the pit over the next few months. I don't remember what triggered it, but one day, the Knife twisted so violently that I fell to the ground in pain. When I finally got to a point where I figured I should get back up, I couldn't move. I was literally paralyzed. I could see my hand from the position I was in and tried to verbally command it to move. It felt like I was shouting, but I'm still not sure if any words actually came out. Either way, it wouldn't budge. I started to think that maybe I'd had a stroke or a heart attack or something and that I was dying—or was already dead.

I don't know how long I lay there, but it seemed like hours. After a while, I slowly regained control of my muscles. It took quite a bit of effort just to stand back up. And when I did, the first thought that popped into my head was that enough was enough.

It was time.

The school year had ended a few weeks prior, and I was all alone in this huge house.

When I bought the razor blades, I figured the cashier might know exactly what I was going to do. I didn't buy anything else. I thought about it, looking intently at a pack of gum. But she was obviously just waiting for the clock to hit the time to go home. I couldn't say I blamed her. Every shitty job I've ever had, I have done the same thing.

I'd seen a few more videos of people shot in the head. None of them looked like it was instant and painless. Fuck that noise. Bleeding out—that was the way to go. It was gradual, just like falling asleep. You'd probably feel a little cold, but that should be the extent of it.

I grabbed the trash can next to my bed as I sat down. No use in bleeding all over the carpet.

The artery. You just nicked the artery, and it was only a matter of time. I took the first blade out of the box and put it in between my right thumb and index finger.

I guess it's that time, I thought.

I put the blade to my left wrist and sliced vertically down.

Nothing happened.

I hadn't pushed hard enough.

I pressed down a bit harder and sliced again. This time, blood trickled to the surface.

Okay, then. All I had to do now was hit the artery in the wrist. It wouldn't take long to bleed out. I just had to keep cutting vertically. That was the right way to do it.

I started to saw into my wrist. I'd press just a little harder every time I thought I had the blade on top of the artery. But something was fucking me up.

There wasn't enough blood.

It should be spouting. Why was it not spouting? I was missing the artery. How did I keep missing it? I changed the angle of blade several times and pushed hard as I sliced. I felt it cut into the tissue. I felt the pressure, but there was no pain really. I heard it cut into the tissue; it sounded like a steak knife cutting gristle. But I kept missing the fucking artery.

How did I keep missing the artery? I was going deep enough. I was sure of it. The blade was a good quarter inch deep into my wrist.

I was going vertical instead of horizontal, as you are supposed to. This was so much harder than movies made it out to be.

I started to lose my cool and sawed like a madman at my wrist.

"Come here, fucker!" I yelled at my artery, as if it might respond.

My phone rang.

It was one or two in the morning. Who the fuck could possibly be calling me right now?

I didn't even look at the screen to see who it was when I answered. "What?"

"Hey."

It was Nicole. Why was she calling me? She didn't want anything to do with me anymore, I'd thought. She'd made that obvious. Did she not realize I knew this?

"Hey?" I said.

"What are you doing?"

I'm curing cancer, I thought to myself. It's the middle of the night—what the fuck do you think I'm doing?

"Why are you calling me?" I asked aloud.

"There's a play this weekend. I was wondering if you wanted to go with me."

"Sure. Provided I stop bleeding by then." Oh shit. Why had I said that? How could I play it off? "I…"

"Why are you bleeding?"

"Um…"

"Why the fuck are you bleeding?"

"Well…"

Dial tone.

Okay. I had finally scared her off. I didn't mean to do it that way, but whatever worked, right?

I grabbed the razor blade and commenced cutting into my wrist again. I'd hit this artery if it was the last thing I did. Hell, I guess it would be the last thing I did.

A pounding on my door.

Ah, shit. I forgot she didn't live but a few blocks away.

"Open the fucking door." It was Nicole's voice. And she sounded pissed. "Open the fucking door!"

"Nah. I'm cool."

From the sound of it, she started putting her shoulder into the door, trying to break it down.

Fuck.

I reluctantly stood up and opened the door. "Don't hurt yourself," I said.

Her eyes went wide when she saw the blood trickling down my wrist. But she turned to leave without another word.

Okay. *Now* I had scared her off.

I shut the door again and went back to probing for the artery in my wrist. I probably would have found it in time if weren't for the alcohol, but the cops in Boulder were quick on the draw. It couldn't have been more than a couple minutes after Nicole stormed off that a police officer was talking at me through the door.

Fuck.

I guessed it was time to take more drastic measures. I looked over at the rifle in my closet. I was just standing up to retrieve it when the voice on the other side of the door said, "If you don't open this door, we're going to have to break it down. And I imagine you are going to be on the line to pay for it. Do you want that?"

Fuck.

Could I muster the strength to shoot myself before they broke down that door? No. There was no way. I had spent hours staring down that barrel, trying to do so. I couldn't imagine that door lasting more than a few seconds. I might not have time to even get to the rifle.

Fine. I walked over to the door and opened it. "Happy, fucker?" I sat back down on the bed and directed the flowing blood from wrist toward the trash can.

"I think you should come with us."

"Yeah? And why is that?" I didn't look up from the blood dripping out of my wrist.

"Because there are people that care about you that want you to."

I let out a brief chuckle. "Oh, yeah? There's people that care about me?" I chuckled again as I ran my thumb down my wrist like a tube of toothpaste, trying to make myself bleed more into the bucket.

"Who do you think called us?"

I know who called you, I thought. Goddamn, I should have just let that girl go. I never should have said word one to her at that party.

"This is just the universe fucking with me."

"Okay. I understand you're in pain. But if you don't come with us willingly, we're going to have to take you by force. Now, I don't want that. And I don't think you want that either. So what do you say?"

"Fine."

I placed the blade on the nightstand and stood up to follow the cops. They led me into a waiting ambulance. Seemed a bit like overkill for the situation, but whatever. I guessed I should give in to the whims of these assholes for a minute.

"Oh, it's just a little baby cut." This came out of the guy assigned to assess my wrist. He wasn't a doctor. Must have been a nurse, I guessed.

Baby cut? I had been literally sawing at my wrist less than a half hour ago. A fake smile crept across my face as I clenched up my other fist, ready to show him a baby cut right to his face, when I felt a firm grip on my clenching arm.

The other nurse didn't have to say anything. She just looked at me and I at her. And I knew from her expression that she was saying, "He's not worth it." And I knew from her grip that she was right. This must not have been the first time the male nurse had let some stupid shit come out of his mouth in her presence.

But that didn't completely calm the urge to punch that thunder douche in his smug face. He disappeared at what was most likely an opportune moment for him, and I'm guessing the nurse that had stopped me from breaking his jaw had also made it apparent he needed to leave.

"So you tried to kill yourself?"

Okay. I had been hoping for at least one semi-intelligent person in this hospital. But now the female nurse I'd thought had some intelligence was asking stupid questions.

"Why?"

Yep. Hospitals were full of nothing but fucking morons. She'd almost made it—but seriously, did she just ask me, "Why?" What kind of answer was she expecting?

"Because I can't stand the thought of never being the world pole-vault champion. It's all I've ever wanted."

"What makes you think you'll never be the pole-vault champion?"

"Are you fucking serious? I was joking. Jesus, just fuck off, will ya?"

I immediately regretted my words. I could see the pain I'd caused in her eyes as she turned away. She didn't deserve that. She was just trying to help me. I was such an asshole.

Ah, well. There was her reason why I tried to kill myself. I was a fucking asshole.

They let me out of the hospital the next day. After that, I tried. I really did.

I signed up for therapy at the college health center. They had me do a little survey. I got assigned a therapist almost immediately after turning it in.

Apparently, I was "extremely suicidal." I didn't know there were different levels.

The therapist I was assigned didn't suck. For the most part, it seemed like she knew what she was talking about. The psychiatrist, the "doctor," on the other hand, was one of the dumbest human beings I'd ever come across.

The fact that I survived those weeks can only be attributed to the therapist. I told that psychiatrist, basically every time I saw him, that the pills he'd prescribed me weren't doing a fucking thing. And without fail, he just kept upping the dosage of the same ineffective pills—even when I specifically asked for something else. I literally told him that the stuff he'd prescribed wasn't helping me at all. Was there something else I could try?

He might as well have said, "Nope, these are the fuck heads that pay my kickbacks, so you are prescribed this and only this. And every time I up your dosage, my kickback gets bigger."

But what he said was the same thing he always said: "Let's try a higher dose and see what that does. Okay?"

Great.

The extent of help for people who were suicidal were greedy assholes peddling pills that didn't work, and judgmental, holier-than-thou jerk offs claiming salvation "if only" you believed the same nonsense that they believed, but especially if you "donated" to their "church."

But I knew that neither pills nor bullshit religion was going to save me.

Nothing was.

I had passed the point of no return. And that was okay. Because I saw it now.

It's hard to describe. But those last few days, as filled with pain as they were, still had an overlying feeling of peace. I'd think about finally ending it, picture my lifeless body, and peace would wrap itself around me like a warm blanket. It was the only thing that made me feel peace.

I dipped further and further with every passing day. I barely had the energy to move anymore. Finally the thought reentered my mind: I can't go on like this.

Nothing happened specifically right before to set me off. Just like with the razor blades, I went to the store and bought only the sleeping pills. And just like before, the cashier didn't bat an eyelash at the fact that it was the only thing I was buying. I'm not trying to blame her. That wasn't her job. And I'm sure they didn't pay her enough for it to be. I think I was just subconsciously hoping that somebody would save me at the last minute, that someone like Superman would just show up and somehow make everything all better. But I think we both know that wasn't even possible. It doesn't happen. Not in real life.

If something was going to happen, I would have to do it myself.

I took the pills out of their packaging and threw them onto a paper plate. It was slow going, as each pill was individually wrapped in one of those annoying punch-out sheets. I figured it wouldn't be as effective if I just popped them out and swallowed them at that pace. I needed to swallow them all at once.

After I finished popping them out, I just left them there on the plate.

It took until the next afternoon.

Blue sky, sunny. It was a beautiful day by all accounts. I could wait a few hours until night—no reason to swallow those pills just yet. I had some beer and some vodka, after all, so I decided I might as well drink them. It was too bad I didn't have any Everclear left.

I think I was also hoping the alcohol would somehow talk me out of it, that the beautiful day and buzz from the booze would make me consider at least postponing my exit from this world—not to mention that Everclear was pretty good at knocking me out. But I just had regular cheap vodka.

And neither it nor the beer had much effect. In fact, as the day turned to night, I was just reminded of how all things end. And the alcohol did nothing but make my head a bit lighter.

It was time.

This assertion was cemented when a friend called me and asked if I wanted to go to a party. I couldn't remember a time when I had said no to that. But I had exactly zero desire to do so. Just the thought of it was painful.

It was definitely time.

I hadn't had any energy for a while now, and just standing up from the couch took some serious effort. Just looking at me, you'd find that hard to believe. I was still ripped from all the boxing I had been doing. I shook the roof of the gym when I hit the heavy bag. But now, standing up from the couch was a struggle.

Maybe there was a part of me that knew what I was about to do and was trying whatever it could to stop me. Maybe I was just broken and knew it. Maybe I knew I was beyond repair.

Either way, I mustered the strength to get up and walk the stairs to my room on the third floor. I didn't time myself, but I couldn't imagine anybody else ever taking that long to walk a couple flights of stairs.

It wasn't reluctance. It was more like I was already dead. And dead people don't move very fast. They don't move at all.

When I finally reached my room, I sat down in front of my computer. I started typing. I typed a paragraph to each person that meant something to me. I told them what they meant and that I was sorry I was not strong enough to defeat this demon plaguing me.

When I finished typing, I grabbed a handful of pills, popped them into my mouth, and chased them down with a swig of vodka. I repeated that until all the pills on that paper plate were gone.

That warm blanket of peace wrapped itself around me again.

I had done it. It was over now. I stood up from the chair and lay down onto the bed. There was a smile on my face when I drifted off to sleep.

All Things End

And that brings us up to now. The story has been told. All of the dominos have fallen.

A choice needs to be made now. A choice between Life and death. I have made my choice and it's time for it to become reality.

I know that the time is near. I can feel myself starting to fade away. It is Adam's time now. I have to die so that he may live—live his Life the way it is supposed to be lived. Truth has been found.

Adam knows. He knows it's time for my journey to come to an end.

"It's time," I say.

Adam just nods. It's not a time for sadness, and he knows this.

Every new beginning comes from some other beginning's end. Enough time has passed that it's morning again. A new beginning from another beginning's end.

I take my last breath as the door of the room opens.

"How are we feeling?" The voice comes from a middle-aged woman I have not seen before. She's probably a shrink. She looks like a shrink.

"Surprisingly excellent."

"That's good to hear. I guess we had a bit of a close call there?"

She's definitely a shrink.

"That's one way to put it."

"How would you put it?"

"Well, I have been doing quite a bit of thinking and reflecting these past few days. I've been having a conversation with myself, so to speak. And this internal dialogue has led me to a new Truth. When I took those pills, it wasn't a cry for help. I took them because I honestly thought they were going to kill me. I genuinely wanted to die. And now, for the first time in as long as I can remember, I don't. I want to live. I have made a decision. It is time to embrace Life and not death."

"Wow. Did you rehearse that?"

I crack a smile. "Maybe a little."

I glance at the chair where I have been imagining myself. The version of myself that has made the argument for Life. The Adam that embraces Life. But the chair is empty now, for I am no longer divided into two sides. The Adam that chooses Life now understands. He has found a new Truth. And there is no more need for the side that has chosen death. That side of me has come to an end.

"All right. Legally, I am allowed to hold you for another couple of days on a psych watch. But I'm getting the feeling that isn't going to be necessary. You seem nothing like what your chart says you were like when you were brought in. I just have to remind you that even though those pills you took were essentially just Benadryl and didn't have acetaminophen in them and weren't immediately lethal, they can still turn your internal organs to mush if you keep ingesting large quantities of them."

I think back to when a nurse finally came in to tell me this not too long ago. I arrived at the hospital in the early morning. I wasn't informed that pills were acetaminophen free until the evening.

"I don't plan on doing anything of the sort ever again. But about that, did it really take an entire day for them to figure out the pills were just Benadryl, or did they just forget to tell me?"

Her facial expression suggests this is the first she is hearing of this.

"It shouldn't have taken them that long. I'm sorry about that, I'm not sure what happened there. I can look into it if you want. It's good to hear you are no longer contemplating suicide and are so enthusiastic about Life. But I also want you to keep seeing your therapist."

"I do plan on that. And no need to look into anything. It's over now."

"Good. Well, I'll sign your release form, and we should have you out of here in fifteen minutes or so. Do you have a ride home?"

"I can call a friend."

"Great. Well, Adam, I hope you don't take this the wrong way, but we hope to never see you here again."

"I couldn't agree with you more."

Life

This part of the story I'm going to call Life. As I walk out of that hospital into the welcoming sunlight, I take a deep breath, close my eyes, tilt my head toward the sky, and soak in the warming rays of the sun.

I can't believe how much color has been restored to the world. Everything around me seems more radiant. Colors are sharper than I can remember. Every smell is more pleasant, every sound more soothing. Later, I'll find that food tastes better than it ever has before.

No. Nobody literally died today. It was just me in that hospital room—two different sides of me. But that side of me that was addicted to misery had to end. I had to let it go. And I had to allow the part of me that most people knew to take over—the part of me that was about fun and Life and wasn't afraid of anything. Because that is the real me.

I'm not that sniveling little shit that made himself miserable on purpose. I refuse to let that be part of my Truth. It was my fault for doing so in the first place.

There is power in that—power in accepting responsibility, power in accepting blame. Because when you realize that you are the one responsible, you realize that only you can fix it. Nobody else can help you until you decide. Because it all comes down to a choice—a choice between Life and death. And I'm not talking about the choice of whether to kill yourself. Breathing doesn't necessarily make you alive. Your heart can be beating, and you can be walking around, but you can still be in the midst of death.

To choose death is to choose nothing. Dead people do nothing. Dead people feel nothing. So I understand why some people would continue to choose death. Dead people never have to answer for their actions. They don't have to accept blame or consequences of any kind.

Choosing Life is harder. It means you have to do things. It means you have to feel things. It means you have to take responsibility for your actions. Choosing Life is choosing hope.

Sometimes you have to remind yourself of your choice. Other people and things can help you, but *you* have to make that choice first, both subconsciously and consciously. And you have to believe in your power to make it happen. You have to know that you are strong enough—because you are. Every human being on Earth is. Everyone has control over one thing, and that is his or her Truth. Only you can define your Truth. And until you do, no amount of church visits, pills, therapy sessions, or even supposedly good things happening in your Life will help. Nobody and nothing can help you until you help yourself first.

You have to choose Life.

Once you do, if it makes it easier to think of depression and addiction as diseases, as things you can fight, then by all means, call them diseases. In the end, it doesn't really matter if your Truth considers them diseases or not. All that matters is your choice. Because if you choose Life, you will fight off the demons in any way you can: thinking of depression as a disease, trying antidepressants, finding God, getting a therapist, talking to loved ones—whatever helps.

Blame is a funny thing. People often try to avoid it, probably because it's painful. It's painful to accept blame. But most don't realize the power inherent in accepting blame, accepting that you've made a mistake, acknowledging your own fault.

Because when you accept that blame, you gain the understanding that the only person truly capable of judging you is yourself. You define your own Truth. Words from other people have near zero effect after that. You become impenetrable. There is nothing anyone else can say that will bother you. There's no insult strong enough to pierce this newfound armor. Just like the old children's rhyme, words really can't hurt you—unless you let them. If you let another person's words affect you, you give up the control to that person. Why would anybody ever do that willingly? Why would anybody let someone else define his or her Truth? And once this realization hits you, that warm blanket wraps itself around you again. You aren't afraid of anything anymore.

On the other side of the coin, people often blame themselves when somebody close to them commits suicide. They think they could have said or done something to prevent it. But they can't blame themselves. People who have ended their own lives are, were, and will always be the ones to blame. They alone have the power to make the choice between Life and death. The only thing anybody else can do is remind them of that choice and hope they choose Life. But they have to make it. They have to decide. Nobody can make that choice for them.

I wish I could say that when I walked out of that hospital I was instantly cured, that I never again had to fight off those thoughts. Those demons. But as with any addiction, relapses are inevitable—and especially dangerous.

Not but a few months later, I started dating a beautiful girl. And that beautiful girl slept with one of my best friends only about a month in. A few years later, I fell in love—legitimately, head over heels, in love. But she didn't. Had these things happened before that day in the hospital, back when I was still choosing death, there's a good chance I wouldn't still be here.

I'm not going to go into some tirade about coping mechanisms and ways to help calm the raging fires of depression and anxiety. Plenty of others have laid that stuff out. You can find that anywhere. And I've tried it all, even pills—anything that I thought might help. Although I'm still on the fence about the pills.

Because that is what you do when you choose Life. You do something. Doing nothing is for dead people.

Maybe there is some Truth to the chemical-imbalance theory. Maybe there isn't. Maybe pills really can help people. Maybe they can't. Maybe. Maybe.

This isn't the story of how I beat back my demons. This isn't a story of redemption. This is just a story of a choice, the most important choice I have ever made, the choice between Life and death.

This is the story of the day I chose Life—and never looked backed.

Nearly ten years after his incarceration, my father was paroled and released from prison. He's still in remission. I can't forgive him for what he did to my sister. I don't have the power to do that. Only she has that power. And I can never excuse what he did. But I can choose to forgive him for the pain he has caused me—not for his sake, but for mine. Carrying around anger and pain is toxic. It cripples your capacity for love. And forgiveness is the only way to purge that. You only have to forgive once, but resentment requires constant work. It also makes it easier that he has turned into one of the best men I have ever known. If you ever doubt that people can change, just take a look at my father. If every man could have the kindness, wisdom, and patience that he has now, the world would be a better place.

My mother remarried and moved to Florida. Right around that same ten-year mark, her second husband died of a heart attack. She has her ups and downs, but she is still the most wonderful mother a man could ever ask for.

My older brother got married and got a good job at a prestigious four-wheel drive workshop in Denver. He's still there—and still one of the best men I know.

My little brother joined what originally seemed a lot like a religious cult to me. But who am I to judge? It seems essentially harmless, makes him happy, and his wife, who even though was technically assigned to him in an arranged marriage, is an absolute sweetheart. He's in real estate, the superlative salesman. I'm still not sure how he does it.

My little sister got married too. She has grown into the best sister a guy could ever ask for, and a wonderful woman. She has also given birth to my favorite little man in world, my nephew—the coolest little kid you'll ever meet.

And me? I started traveling. I did my best to *do something*. Because that's what you do when you choose Life. You live. I still haven't met the one, if there is such a thing. But that's okay. And if I never do, it'll still be okay. Choosing Life also means accepting everything that happens—everything Life gives you, everything it doesn't, everything it shows you and surprises you with, everything it takes away.

I know it's ridiculous, but deep down, I'd still like to be like Superman. And I know it will never happen. But who knows? Maybe one day I'll be lucky enough to have a daughter. And just maybe, if I can be a good enough man and father, I could be Superman in her eyes. That would be more than enough for me. But even if that doesn't happen, I'll be okay. Because I've chosen Life— and all the good, bad, and ugly that go with it.

Even now, nearly fifteen years later, I still have relapses here and there where I have to beat back besieging demons. But the battles have become much fewer and farther between—and easier and easier to win. I haven't once considered changing my choice. But all of that is another story entirely.

After all, this isn't the end.

It is merely…

The Beginning

CPSIA information can be obtained
at www.ICGtesting.com
Printed in the USA
FFOW03n0654080218
45002116-45299FF